*A Diary*

*of*

*Edinburgh*

# A·DIARY·OF EDINBURGH

Written by TREVOR ROYLE
Illustrated by RICHARD DEMARCO

POLYGON BOOKS

ISBN 0 904919 52 8

First published 1981 by
Polygon Books,
1 Buccleuch Place,
Edinburgh, EH8 9LW.

Typeset in Bembo by
Edinburgh University Student Publications Board,
1 Buccleuch Place,
Edinburgh, EH8 9LW.

Reproduced from copy supplied,
printed and bound in Great Britain by
Billing and Sons,
Guildford, London, Oxford, Worcester.

# Introduction

This is a diary of the main historical events that have shaped the course of Edinburgh's story from the beginnings of recorded history to the present day. It is not a history of the city, neither is it a survey of the major events and personalities, although these, too, have their parts to play within the diary's pages. Rather it is a book of days, a day-to-day record of the city's past. Some of the events recorded here belong, perhaps more properly, to the annals of Scottish or British history, such as the birth of King James VI of Scotland and I of England on 19th June 1566 or the beginning of Gladstone's successful Midlothian campaign on 31st March 1880. Others are more domestic, the detritus of everyday life: we glimpse into the pages of the surgeon, Thomas Kincaid's private diary for 11th December 1687, and share the sorrow of Sir Walter Scott's ruin a few days later on 18th December 1825. Great people come and go across the pages of the year and as well as Scott, other names from Scotland's history have helped to form the story of Edinburgh: Robert Burns, Robert Louis Stevenson, Lord Kames and Lord Monboddo, David Hume, Adam Smith, John Maclean, the poets Gavin Douglas, Allan Ramsay and Robert Fergusson, architects and artists like Sir Henry Raeburn and Robert Adam. And in their midst are the recollections of famous visitors, people like Washington Irving, Oliver Goldsmith, G. K. Chesterton and Dorothy Wordsworth.

Throughout it all, though, runs the minutiae of the governance of the city of Edinburgh. From its Royal Charter granted on 28th May 1329 Edinburgh has been one of the principal cities of Scotland and when the Stewarts became monarchs it became their capital, a title it keeps to this day. Its administration was left in the hands of the merchant guilds and from the records of the Town Council a vivid picture emerges of the medieval city that was not to change its shape in any significant way until the construction of the Georgian new town in the late eighteenth century. From the pages of Edinburgh's recorded civic history several themes recur over the years. An inability to curb plague and other horrifyingly contagious diseases is mentioned on 17th January 1513 and again on 2nd August 1530. Its appearance was no doubt due to the dirt and squalor of Edinburgh's narrow closes and wynds and to the notorious habit of throwing all manner of household rubbish into the streets below. Little wonder that on his visit to Edinburgh in August 1773 Dr Johnson should have remarked to James Boswell that he could smell him in the dark.

Nastiness of another kind was manifested in the edicts of 17th November 1587 and the 9th December 1767 against the theatre and other public entertainments, and although Edinburgh is now a leading cultural centre with its international Festival and handful of theatres and galleries, the city fathers have had a habit of thundering against the wickedness of the theatre. Similarly vice, prostitution and drunkenness has long flourished and hardly a century seems to have passed without futile steps being taken to eradicate their reoccurrence.

Crime, too, prospered in the fetid streets of the old town and as well as the spectacular story of Deacon Brodie, respectable citizen and member of the Town Council by day, housebreaker and robber by night (see 1st October 1788), Edinburgh has spawned its share of greedy, stupid, yet undoubtedly sad criminals: Burke and Hare, the murderers (28th January 1829), the poisoner Eugene Chantrelle (31st May 1878), and Jessie King and the slaughter of the innocents (11th March 1889).

But set against these failings, which are the property, too, of any major city, Edinburgh has also been an unrivalled centre of learning and innovation. The philosopher David Hume lived in the city, Adam Smith, the economist and author of *The Wealth of Nations*, lies buried in the Canongate churchyard, it was here that Simpson discovered the anaesthetic properties of chloroform, Edinburgh's was one of the first properly equipped municipal fire brigades, James Clerk Maxwell, the "father of modern science", owed his early education to Edinburgh Academy, and Napier of Merchiston fashioned the logarithmic tables. Publishing and printing were once two of the city's greatest industries and the Edinburgh families of McEwan and Younger were the brewers of some of the finest beers created by man. Sibbald and the Botanic Gardens (7th July 1675), Drummond and the construction of the New Town (17th April 1767), Patrick Geddes and the concept of modern town and country planning (11th August 1931), Kemp's Scott Monument (17th August 1846) and the construction of modern hospitals making Edinburgh an international centre for medical research (the City Hospital on 13th May 1903, Craighouse on 16th July 1890, the Royal Infirmary on 6th August 1729, Princess Margaret Rose on 2nd October 1929 and the Royal Hospital for Sick Children on 31st November 1895), together with the great writers, law lords and thinkers, all these have combined to make Edinburgh what it is, one of the great European cities.

In making the selection of dates I have been greatly assisted by consulting the *Minutes and Records of the Town Council of Edinburgh*, the *Books of the Old Edinburgh Club* (1908-) and the files of *The Scotsman*, and the Edinburgh Room of the City Library has been a mine of information wherein rich seams of help and advice are to be found. Its carefully filed papers and press-cuttings have been invaluable to me as has the uncanny ability of the staff to discover seemingly

*Edinburgh from Salisbury Crags*

irretrievable facts about the city and its past. Other books consulted and which continue to offer the most broadly based reading on Edinburgh are: Charles Boog Watson, *Notes on the Closes and Wynds of Edinburgh*, Edinburgh, 1923; E. F. Catford, *Edinburgh: The Story of a City*, London, 1975; Robert Chambers, *Traditions of Edinburgh*, Edinburgh, 1825; David Daiches, *Edinburgh*, London, 1978; James Grant, *Old and New Edinburgh*, 3 vols., London, 1883; John Mackay, *History of the Burgh of Canongate*, Edinburgh, 1886; William Maitland, *The History of Edinburgh from its Foundation to the Present Time*, Edinburgh, 1753; Charles J. Smith, *Historic South Edinburgh*, 2 vols., Edinburgh, 1979; Sir Daniel Wilson, *Memorials of Edinburgh in Olden Times*, Edinburgh and London, 1891.

I owe a debt of gratitude to Liz Ewan of the Department of Scottish History for her most useful comments on the text and her suggestions for its improvement, although, of course, all errors remain my responsibility. Richard Demarco (28th August 1966) provided a series of splendid, evocative drawings, proving yet again that Edinburgh owes him more than just thanks; and my publishers, who suggested the idea in the first place, insisted, and then ensured, that the compilation of this book of Edinburgh days should be an agreeable, far-from-onerous task. I hope that something of our pleasure makes itself felt as the year in historical Edinburgh unfolds, day by single day.

TREVOR ROYLE
*Edinburgh, October 1981.*


*****


The drawings which are included within represent a distinctly personal viewpoint. More often than not they focus on what I call "the small and secret spaces". They are of the nooks, crannies and corners which delight and surprise the visitor who is prepared to make a pedestrian exploration. They emphasise the need to make a journey through Edinburgh's townscape.

Every drawing was done in autumn 1981, during the months of September and October, and they are the result of a 500-mile tour of the city. The medium is pen and ink, deliberately chosen to emphasise the sculptural nature of a city I see as a northern equivalent of Florence.

RICHARD DEMARCO
*Edinburgh, October 1981.*

*Advocates' Close*

# 1982

## January
```
M    4 11 18 25
T    5 12 19 26
W    6 13 20 27
Th   7 14 21 28
F  1 8 15 22 29
S  2 9 16 23 30
Sun 3 10 17 24 31
```

## February
```
M  1 8 15 22
T  2 9 16 23
W  3 10 17 24
Th 4 11 18 25
F  5 12 19 26
S  6 13 20 27
Sun 7 14 21 28
```

## March
```
M  1 8 15 22 29
T  2 9 16 23 30
W  3 10 17 24 31
Th 4 11 18 25
F  5 12 19 26
S  6 13 20 27
Sun 7 14 21 28
```

## April
```
M    5 12 19 26
T    6 13 20 27
W    7 14 21 28
Th 1 8 15 22 29
F  2 9 16 23 30
S  3 10 17 24
Sun 4 11 18 25
```

## May
```
M    3 10 17 24 31
T    4 11 18 25
W    5 12 19 26
Th   6 13 20 27
F    7 14 21 28
S  1 8 15 22 29
Sun 2 9 16 23 30
```

## June
```
M    7 14 21 28
T  1 8 15 22 29
W  2 9 16 23 30
Th 3 10 17 24
F  4 11 18 25
S  5 12 19 26
Sun 6 13 20 27
```

## July
```
M    5 12 19 26
T    6 13 20 27
W    7 14 21 28
Th 1 8 15 22 29
F  2 9 16 23 30
S  3 10 17 24 31
Sun 4 11 18 25
```

## August
```
M  2 9 16 23 30
T  3 10 17 24 31
W  4 11 18 25
Th 5 12 19 26
F  6 13 20 27
S  7 14 21 28
Sun 1 8 15 22 29
```

## September
```
M    6 13 20 27
T    7 14 21 28
W  1 8 15 22 29
Th 2 9 16 23 30
F  3 10 17 24
S  4 11 18 25
Sun 5 12 19 26
```

## October
```
M    4 11 18 25
T    5 12 19 26
W    6 13 20 27
Th   7 14 21 28
F  1 8 15 22 29
S  2 9 16 23 30
Sun 3 10 17 24 31
```

## November
```
M  1 8 15 22 29
T  2 9 16 23 30
W  3 10 17 24
Th 4 11 18 25
F  5 12 19 26
S  6 13 20 27
Sun 7 14 21 28
```

## December
```
M    6 13 20 27
T    7 14 21 28
W  1 8 15 22 29
Th 2 9 16 23 30
F  3 10 17 24 31
S  4 11 18 25
Sun 5 12 19 26
```

# 1983

## January

| M | 3 | 10 | 17 | 24 | 31 |
|---|---|----|----|----|----|
| T | 4 | 11 | 18 | 25 | |
| W | 5 | 12 | 19 | 26 | |
| Th | 6 | 13 | 20 | 27 | |
| F | 7 | 14 | 21 | 28 | |
| S | 1 | 8 | 15 | 22 | 29 |
| Sun | 2 | 9 | 16 | 23 | 30 |

## February

| M | | 7 | 14 | 21 | 28 |
|---|---|---|----|----|----|
| T | 1 | 8 | 15 | 22 | |
| W | 2 | 9 | 16 | 23 | |
| Th | 3 | 10 | 17 | 24 | |
| F | 4 | 11 | 18 | 25 | |
| S | 5 | 12 | 19 | 26 | |
| Sun | 6 | 13 | 20 | 27 | |

## March

| M | | 7 | 14 | 21 | 28 |
|---|---|---|----|----|----|
| T | 1 | 8 | 15 | 22 | 29 |
| W | 2 | 9 | 16 | 23 | 30 |
| Th | 3 | 10 | 17 | 24 | 31 |
| F | 4 | 11 | 18 | 25 | |
| S | 5 | 12 | 19 | 26 | |
| Sun | 6 | 13 | 20 | 27 | |

## April

| M | | 4 | 11 | 18 | 25 |
|---|---|---|----|----|----|
| T | | 5 | 12 | 19 | 26 |
| W | | 6 | 13 | 20 | 27 |
| Th | | 7 | 14 | 21 | 28 |
| F | 1 | 8 | 15 | 22 | 29 |
| S | 2 | 9 | 16 | 23 | 30 |
| Sun | 3 | 10 | 17 | 24 | |

## May

| M | 2 | 9 | 16 | 23 | 30 |
|---|---|---|----|----|----|
| T | 3 | 10 | 17 | 24 | 31 |
| W | 4 | 11 | 18 | 25 | |
| Th | 5 | 12 | 19 | 26 | |
| F | 6 | 13 | 20 | 27 | |
| S | 7 | 14 | 21 | 28 | |
| Sun | 1 | 8 | 15 | 22 | 29 |

## June

| M | | 6 | 13 | 20 | 27 |
|---|---|---|----|----|----|
| T | | 7 | 14 | 21 | 28 |
| W | 1 | 8 | 15 | 22 | 29 |
| Th | 2 | 9 | 16 | 23 | 30 |
| F | 3 | 10 | 17 | 24 | |
| S | 4 | 11 | 18 | 25 | |
| Sun | 5 | 12 | 19 | 26 | |

## July

| M | | 4 | 11 | 18 | 25 |
|---|---|---|----|----|----|
| T | | 5 | 12 | 19 | 26 |
| W | | 6 | 13 | 20 | 27 |
| Th | | 7 | 14 | 21 | 28 |
| F | 1 | 8 | 15 | 22 | 29 |
| S | 2 | 9 | 16 | 23 | 30 |
| Sun | 3 | 10 | 17 | 24 | 31 |

## August

| M | 1 | 8 | 15 | 22 | 29 |
|---|---|---|----|----|----|
| T | 2 | 9 | 16 | 23 | 30 |
| W | 3 | 10 | 17 | 24 | 31 |
| Th | 4 | 11 | 18 | 25 | |
| F | 5 | 12 | 19 | 26 | |
| S | 6 | 13 | 20 | 27 | |
| Sun | 7 | 14 | 21 | 28 | |

## September

| M | 5 | 12 | 19 | 26 |
|---|---|----|----|----|
| T | 6 | 13 | 20 | 27 |
| W | 7 | 14 | 21 | 28 |
| Th | 1 | 8 | 15 | 22 | 29 |
| F | 2 | 9 | 16 | 23 | 30 |
| S | 3 | 10 | 17 | 24 | |
| Sun | 4 | 11 | 18 | 25 | |

## October

| M | | 3 | 10 | 17 | 24 | 31 |
|---|---|---|----|----|----|----|
| T | | 4 | 11 | 18 | 25 | |
| W | | 5 | 12 | 19 | 26 | |
| Th | | 6 | 13 | 20 | 27 | |
| F | | 7 | 14 | 21 | 28 | |
| S | 1 | 8 | 15 | 22 | 29 | |
| Sun | 2 | 9 | 16 | 23 | 30 | |

## November

| M | | 7 | 14 | 21 | 28 |
|---|---|---|----|----|----|
| T | 1 | 8 | 15 | 22 | 29 |
| W | 2 | 9 | 16 | 23 | 30 |
| Th | 3 | 10 | 17 | 24 | |
| F | 4 | 11 | 18 | 25 | |
| S | 5 | 12 | 19 | 26 | |
| Sun | 6 | 13 | 20 | 27 | |

## December

| M | | 5 | 12 | 19 | 26 |
|---|---|---|----|----|----|
| T | | 6 | 13 | 20 | 27 |
| W | | 7 | 14 | 21 | 28 |
| Th | 1 | 8 | 15 | 22 | 29 |
| F | 2 | 9 | 16 | 23 | 30 |
| S | 3 | 10 | 17 | 24 | 31 |
| Sun | 4 | 11 | 18 | 25 | |

# January

From its craggy rock where it stands sentinel over the medieval town, the Castle dominates the skyline of Edinburgh. There has been a fortress on the rock since the fourteenth century.

# January

1st _____

2nd _____

3rd _____

# January

## 1st

**1600:** New Year's Day was changed from 25th March to bring it within the Twelve Days of Yule, or "Daft Days" as they were known in Edinburgh. The folklorist F. Marian McNeill described a traditional New Year celebration outside the Tron Kirk in the High Street in *The Silver Bough* (1961). "Here and there, groups of young people, some in carnival hats, some in complete disguise, and equipped with long feathers, blow-outs, tambourines and bells are dancing and singing and throwing coloured streamers riotously around. Barrows of oranges and the windows of the fruit and sweet shops that have remained open all night make oases of colour and gaiety in the dark northern light. Hip bottles are freely proffered... then suddenly a roar rises from the myriad throats; the bells peel forth, the sirens scream: the New Year is born!"

## 2nd

**1963:** The Traverse Theatre opened its first home at James Court off the Lawnmarket with a double bill, *Orison* by Fernando Arrabal and *Huis Clos* by Jean Paul Sartre. That first performance was described by *The Scotsman*'s drama critic as being a sensation similar to having "a lion in your lap", and the Traverse quickly established itself as one of the world's leading avant garde theatres with a reputation for staging new and imaginative work. It had its origins in the 1962 Festival Fringe when a group of enthusiasts saw the need to establish a year-round theatre event in the city and they persuaded Tom Mitchell, the owner of the James Court premises, formerly Kelly's Paradise, a notorious brothel, to lease them the building. In 1969 the Traverse moved to the Grassmarket.

## 3rd

**1867:** Writing from Mentone in the south of France, Thomas Carlyle reminisced about his first view of Parliament Hall in the High Street, the traditional meeting place for advocates and their clients. "An immense Hall, dimly lighted from the top of the walls, and perhaps with candles burning in it here and there; all in strange *chiaroscuro*, and filled with what I thought (exaggeratively) a thousand or two of human creatures; all astir in a boundless buzz of talk, and simmering about in every direction, some solitary, some in groups. By degrees I noticed that some were in wig and black gown, some not, but in common clothes, all well-dressed; that here and there on the sides of the Hall were little thrones with enclosures and steps leading up; red velvet figures sitting in said thrones, and the black gowned eagerly speaking to them. . . ."

# January

4th _____

5th _____

6th _____

# January

## 4th

**1739:** From the middle of the eighteenth century Edinburgh was plagued by bodysnatchers, or resurrectionists as they were more commonly known, who would rob graves of their newly dead bodies and then sell them to doctors for medical research. The minutes of the parish church register of South Leith Church, which once maintained the largest cemetery in Leith, gives vivid witness to the chillingly retold stories of carts and vans rattling along cobbled streets carrying their freight of newly disinterred corpses. Several measures were tried out to prevent this gruesome practice, the most effective being the construction of a watchtower with watchmen. A later minute complained of "much disturbance made" by the watchmen, and they were banned from bringing "too much liquor more than is necessary for their refreshment".

## 5th

**1694:** The old Edinburgh city Bedlam had as one of its last inhabitants an indigent student who had fallen on evil times. Four years later it moved to a new building in South Greyfriars yard near present-day Forrest Road. The student's upkeep was met by the Town Council: "Anent ane petition given in be Mr Gilbert Rule and Mr Thomas Wilkie ministers of this city shewing that where they did indgage Alexr Watson keeper of the Correction house to take under his custody and caire Archibald Campbell a poor student at the Colledge who had fallen in a distraction and since into a perfect stupidity that he can doe nothing for himself and promised 3 sh. scots a day to the said Alexr Watsone Which since May was a year they had endevored to paye except twenty pounds Scots which is yit due. . . ." The Council paid.

## 6th

**1564:** On Uphalieday, or Twelfth Night, the Christian feast of Epiphany, Mary Fleming, one of Mary Queen of Scots' "Four Maries", was selected as the Queen of Bean, or Queen of the Revels, in the Palace of Holyroodhouse. A bean was hidden in a fruitcake and whoever received the slice of cake concealing the bean became the leader of the revels which included a mock coronation, mummery and games of forfeits. Mary Queen of Scots entered into the spirit of the occasion, abdicating in favour of the sovereign for the day and taking part in the mock coronation. Uphalieday brought to an end the twelve days of Christmas, a period that was known in Edinburgh as the "Daft Days", and it was for many years the one recognised annual holiday. Its celebration continued until the early nineteenth century.

# January

7th _____

8th _____

9th _____

# January

## 7th

**1758:** The poet Allan Ramsay died in his house on Castlehill which was dubbed the "Goose Pie" by local wags. During his long career in Edinburgh Ramsay had been a bookseller in Niddry's Wynd, in the High Street and at the east end of the Luckenbooths, and he is credited with starting the first lending library in Britain. One of his poems, "Elegy on Maggy Johnston", recounts the dangers of drinking too much after a game of golf.

> *Fou closs we us'd to drink and rant,*
> *Until we did baith glowre and gaunt,*
> *And pish and spew, and yesk and maunt,*
> *Right swash I true;*
> *Then of auld stories we did cant*
> *Whan we were fou.*

## 8th

**1747:** According to William Forbes, a burgess of the city, the close in the High Street that we know as South Gray's Close, was known as "Coinyie Close" or the close where coins were minted. Until its demolition in 1877 the Royal Mint or Cunyie House stood at the foot of the close and in his will George Heriot, the sixteenth-century goldsmith, referred to the "venall callit Gray's Clois or Coynehous cloise". It was known as Gray's Close —the "south" was added later to distinguish it from another close of the same name on the north side of the High Street— from a charter of 1512 which mentioned one John Gray as the owner of the titles and as late as the eighteenth century there was still a Janet Gray living in one of the tenements within the close.

## 9th

**1935:** Following speculation about the future of Bruntsfield House, its owner Sir Victor Warrender agreed to make over this historic property to the city at a cost of £22,000. The lands of Bruntsfield derive from a fourteenth-century Broune, who was the King's Sergeant of the Burgh Muir, and a manor house on Broune's Field has probably stood there for several centuries. Towards the end of the seventeenth century the Warrenders became associated with the area and the family names are still continued in the names of the neighbouring streets: Thirlestane, Lauderdale and Spottiswoode. Little was done to enhance Bruntsfield House until, in 1963, it became the centre piece of the new James Gillespie's School for Girls, inspiring the setting of Muriel Spark's *The Prime of Miss Jean Brodie.*

# January

10th _____

11th _____

12th _____

# January

## 10th

**1886:** Heriot-Watt College, which became Edinburgh's second university in 1965, came into being as a result of the amalgamation of the endowments of the Watt Institute with those of George Heriot's Hospital. The Institution had been founded in 1821 as a School of Arts and Mechanics' Institute in Niddry Street. In 1874 it acquired a new name in honour of the Scottish inventor James Watt and moved to more spacious accommodation in Chambers Street opposite the Royal Scottish Museum. Much of Heriot-Watt University is now housed on the outskirts of Edinburgh at Riccarton, near the suburb of Currie, and it has maintained its worldwide reputation for offering a wide range of degree courses in the sciences and in engineering.

## 11th

**1681:** The original Prestonfield House, which stands in the suburb of Newington, on the southern side of Arthur's Seat, was burned down by students of the University of Edinburgh, who suspected its owner, Sir James Dick, of Catholic tendencies. Dick was Lord Provost at the time and as a close friend of the Duke of Albany and York he enjoyed considerable political power. The house as it exists today, was rebuilt at the expense of the Scottish Treasury and in 1773 the next owner, Sir Alexander Dick, President of the Royal College of Edinburgh, entertained James Boswell and Dr Samuel Johnson during the latter's visit to the city. The house has since had several owners and it is now a luxury hotel with a restaurant that has won acclaim for the high standards of its cuisine.

## 12th

**1770:** The account books of Mrs Ross of Pitcalnie, an indefatigable collector of bills and odd bits of paper, show payment of £20.11.5$\frac{1}{2}$ to her cabinetmaker, one William Brodie, the notorious Deacon of Wrights who led a double life of respectable citizen by day and daring robber by night. Following the death of her husband, Mrs Ross took rooms in Brodie's Close in the Lawnmarket which were found for her by a friend of her son Murdo: "It consists only of three rooms and a kitchen which Mama thinks will answer you very well. . . ." Brodie's father, Francis, had started the business after being admitted as a burgess in 1735 and had announced it as "at Palladio's Head in the lawnmarket" thereby stating his intention to create inexpensive yet elegant furniture in the fashionable neo-classical style.

# January

13th _____

14th _____

15th _____

# January

## 13th

**1865:** The Theatre Royal in Broughton Street which had been prone to several accidents during its career, was burned down causing considerable damage to the locality. The theatre had been open for the most of the century and it had operated under a variety of names. It reopened later under the ownership of R. H. Wyndham who also had the lease of the old Theatre Royal in Shakespeare Square at the east end of Princes Street which was demolished to make way for the General Post Office. Under Wyndham's management the Broughton Street theatre became renowned for its pantomimes which were presented twice daily during the Christmas season. "Many still sigh for a return of those days of the gorgeous transformation scene, followed by clown, pantaloon, harlequin and columbine . . ." reported an anonymous theatregoer in 1926.

## 14th

**1831:** Henry Mackenzie, a writer whose life spanned the two great ages of Edinburgh literary life — the Enlightenment and the reign of Sir Walter Scott — died at his home in Edinburgh, aged seventy-six. Although he only wrote one notable novel, the sentimental *Man of Feeling* (which was also his nickname), he had a considerable influence on many a young writer, and Scott's biographer, John Gibson Lockhart, has left us with this description of him: "In the countenance of Mackenzie there is the clear transparency of skin, the freshness of complexion, in the midst of all the extenuation of old age. The wrinkles, too, are set close to each other, line upon line; not deep and bold, and rugged like those of most old men, but equal and undivided over the whole surface, as if no touch but that of time had been there."

## 15th

**1686:** James Aitkenhead successfully petitioned the Town Council to become keeper of the Netherbow Port, one of the main entrances to the city, because his father who had been keeper was "seekly and unable to attend upon that charge". The Netherbow Port, which stood at the present junction of the High Street and Jeffrey Street, and is marked by brass plates set in the roadway, was an arched gateway with a tower and a spire and it was built in 1513 at the place where the city wall divided Edinburgh from the Canongate. Damaged in 1544 when an English army invaded Edinburgh, it was rebuilt and stood until 1764 when it made way for a more direct route to the Canongate. It was the custom to place the heads of criminals on spikes above the main gate.

# January

16th _____

17th _____

18th _____

# January

## 16th

**1909:** The first whale to be caught by the Leith-based firm of Christian Salvesen was killed in the Antarctic Ocean by gunner Edmund Paulson. Although initial catches were below expectations, the company continued to exploit their part in the new industry and by 1911 they were the largest whaling company in the world. The Salvesens came originally from Norway and had opened their first place of business in Grangemouth in 1843, moving later to Leith which had become their base for whaling, conducted initially (1899) in the North Atlantic. Whaling continued to be associated with Leith until the nineteen-fifities when international agreements gave a greater degree of protection to whales and hunting them became a less valid financial proposition for the Salvesen company.

## 17th

**1513:** Plague was one of the most unwelcome visitors to Edinburgh during the medieval period and outbreaks were reported well into the seventeenth century. That it was more than a task for the Town Council's exhortations can be seen in this edict from King James IV in Holyroodhouse: "James be the grace of God king of Scottis to the provest and baillies of our burgh of Edinburgh greting: Wit ye that with the avys of our counsale for stancheing of the contagious plaige of pestilence now ringing in dyuers places within this our realm, and be Goddis grace to escew siclyk and apperand caus of the samyn in tyme cuming, safer as may be done with diligence of men, hes deuysit thir statutis and rewlis to be maid and keipit within the boundis of your office. . . ."

## 18th

**1832:** According to the minutes of the Town Council the property in Bull's Close off the Canongate had been bought by a lint manufacturer called Peter Lamont and were to be known in consequence as Lamont's Land. The original owner, who had given his name to the close and to the lands, was a burgess of the city called Robert Bull. He had come into the property through his marriage to the second daughter of John Wright but the close has enjoyed several names during its long history. In the late eighteenth century it was known as Drummond's Close from one of its inhabitants, Mary Drummond, the sister of the famous Lord Provost of Edinburgh, Sir George Drummond. She was also a renowned Quaker and a friend of Alexander Pope. Another name was Ford's Row from the houses owned by Ford's Glassworks.

# January

19th _____

20th _____

21st _____

# January

19th _____

**1681:** The Town Council ordered a collection to be made in all of Edinburgh's churches as a contribution to a fund which had been established to pay the ransoms of four seamen taken prisoner by the Turks. The men had been captured "in the straits by ane privat of Algiers many moneths agoe. Since that tyme they have remained in most miserable bondage and slavery of those infidells being fettered in irons and getting scarse sustenation for ther mentinànce not having any means to ransome or procure ther relief as may apear by severall letters under the suplicants hands and severall of the petitioners having maid application to the lords of his Majesties privie councill for a warrand towards a voluntar contribution to be made in order to save ther releisment."

20th _____

**1660:** A committee of the Town Council was convened to inspect the roof of the Tron Kirk in the High Street to discover if it should be covered with lead. It took them roughly three years to come to the conclusion that it was possible to remove the original copper and slates and to renew the roof with "leid with all convenience in the most frugall way they can". The Tron Church was built in the reign of King Charles I and it took its name from the "tron" or public weighbridge which stood nearby. Although of rather nondescript style it boasted a fine wooden spire which was destroyed in the great fire of 1824 when the same lead cascaded in molten balls on to the fire fighters below. Closed for worship in 1952 the future of the restored church is still undecided.

21st_____

**1575:** Alexander Clark was presented with a licence to complete the constructions of buildings in Niddry's Wynd, a narrow street that joined the High Street to the Cowgate where South Bridge now stands. The present Niddry Street is further east than the original due to changes made during the construction of the two bridges. The wynd was probably named after Robert Niddry, a city magistrate during the fifteenth century, and is thought to have contained the town house of the Wauchopes of Niddry. According to Chambers in his *Traditions of Edinburgh*, the wynd "abounded in curious antique houses many of which had been the residences of remarkable persons". It was there that the poet Allan Ramsay opened his bookseller's shop before moving to later premises in the High Street.

# January

22nd _____

23rd _____

24th _____

# January

## 22nd

**1732:** A party of Highlanders wearing the livery of Lord Lovat forced their way into the lodgings of Lady Grange and forcibly seized her. From Edinburgh the party made its way to the West Highlands, finally ending up on the island of Heskir near Skye where she was detained for two years. She was the estranged wife of the Jacobite Lord Grange and after their marriage had ended she tried on several occasions to gain her revenge by denouncing him to the government, and her drunken ragings at him in the streets of the old town were the talk of Edinburgh. To protect himself and his cause Grange was forced to take the drastic step of kidnapping his wife and incarcerating her in the Western Highlands. In 1734 she was transferred to the more remote island of St Kilda where she died in 1745.

## 23rd

**1779:** One of the most respected publishers of the eighteenth century Enlightenment was William Creech whose breakfast room in Craig's Close became a meeting place for literary discussions known as "Creech's Levees". He first published Henry Mackenzie's *The Mirror*, a magazine, on this date, which was based on the London-published *Spectator* and in later life Mackenzie was dubbed "our Scottish Addison" by Sir Walter Scott. Although the magazine attracted some of the ablest minds in Edinburgh it was not a success and when it ceased publication in December Mackenzie blamed "the fastidiousness with which in a place so narrow as Edinburgh, home productions are commonly received". A later magazine, *The Lounger*, was no more successful than its predecessor.

## 24th

**1695:** The Kirk Session of Leith, pleading poverty, proclaimed that the burial of the poor of the parish in plain wooden caskets should be discontinued and that instead use was to be made of a simple wooden bier. This would probably have been a rough hinged casket with sides that could be let down to allow the body to slip into the grave and it was to be used for all the poor except "such persons as have been some considerable note and credit to the place and are fallen back". Following the Reformation, funerals were simple affairs as the church was anxious to reject any ceremony that smacked of superstition and it was not until the early years of the nineteenth century that ministers again attended on these solemn occasions to offer spiritual comfort to mourners.

# January

25th _____

26th _____

27th _____

# January

25th _____

**1817:** *The Scotsman* newspaper was first published on the day which is celebrated by Scots all over the world as the birthdate of Robert Burns. It had been founded the previous year by Charles Maclaren, a Customs House official, and William Ritchie, a lawyer. They were joined later by John Ramsay McCulloch, an economist. The newspaper espoused the Whig political cause and it was an enthusiastic supporter of Catholic emancipation and the Reform Bill of 1832. *The Scotsman* has since been owned by several proprietors, most notably the Canadian Roy Thomson (later Lord Thomson of Fleet) who purchased it in 1953. The newspaper's original office was in 257 High Street and in 1905 it moved to its present headquarters on the North Bridge.

26th _____

**1666:** Although the baking of bread had long been associated with the Dean Village beside the Water of Leith, many families continued to do their own baking at home, often causing disastrous fires in the narrow confines of the tenements of the old town. A Town Council edict proclaimed a fine of a hundred merks for anyone found baking bread "in any high or loftit houses", instead of "laich cellars or voltis upon the ground". Flour for the city's needs was also ground in the Dean Village and the granary still stands at the foot of Bell's Brae with its function self-evident in a panel displaying the tools of the craft of the miller and the baker. During the nineteenth century, Dean Village was the scene of much philanthropic reconstruction of its older buildings.

27th _____

**1590:** At a trial in the High Court the so-called "Witches of North Berwick" confessed their sins against the King, James VI, during his sea voyage to Denmark to meet and marry his future Queen, the Danish Princess Ann. It was stated that the witches tried to bring about the destruction at sea of the King's entourage in a furious hurricane, and that their means of execution was through the intervention of the Devil who appeared wearing a "black gown with a black hat on his head" and with "claws on his hands and feet like the griffon". The witches used other measures too, including the baptism of a black cat which was then cast into the sea from Leith Pier. Despite these measures and the natural storminess of the North Sea, James survived the voyage, something the witches failed to do at their trial.

# January

28th _____

29th _____

30th _____

# January

## 28th

**1829:** Edinburgh could only talk about one event: William Burke had been hanged. In 1827 Burke and his accomplice William Hare had formed one of the most despicable and yet oddly picturesque criminal partnerships in Edinburgh's long history, by murdering up to sixteen people to supply corpses for the distinguished anatomist, Dr Knox. Having sold the corpse of a lodger to defray his debts, they turned to the more reliable business of murder so that the doctor might be supplied by a steady flow of suitable corpses, and the revelation of their crimes caused a sensation in the city. Against a background of public hysteria the two men were put on trial only for Hare to turn King's evidence and for Burke to devote most of his defence to the exculpation of his mistress, Helen MacDougall. Burke was sentenced to death and hanged.

## 29th

**1517:** A Papal Bull granted by Pope Leo X established the convent of St Catherine of Siena as a benefit "to the whole people of Scotland". The sisters took over the chapel of St John the Baptist which had been founded by Sir John Crauford in the area to the south-east of the Meadows and gradually it came to be known as Sciennes from the name of the order of the convent. Several of the nuns were widows of those killed at the Battle of Flodden including Lady Jane Hepburn, the widow of the Earl of Seton, a close friend of James IV. Although the convent did not have a long lifetime — it was burned by Hertford's English army in 1544 and wasted during the Reformation — the nuns had a reputation for piety and austerity, virtues that were often lacking in the Renaissance church.

## 30th

**1684:** Following a petition by William Carmichael, merchant of Edinburgh, the Town Council agreed to renew the lease of his shop in the Luckenbooths for an annual rent of £80 Scots and added the proviso that the lease would be null and void if the Luckenbooths were to be demolished. These locked booths which had been built about 1460 were a singular feature of the High Street opposite the High Church of St Giles. In the seven tenements from four to six storeys high the shops were at street level while the merchants had their dwellings in the houses above. Below the south wall of the Luckenbooths and St Giles was a narrow passage called the Krames, where traders without shops could offer their wares from stands. The Luckenbooths were finally taken down between 1817 and 1818.

# January

31st_____

**1820:** The ratification by the Town Council of the appointment
of Robert Graham to the vacant Chair of Botany within the
University fulfilled the hopes expressed earlier that month in the
*Edinburgh Evening Courant* that the new professor would
superintend and manage the new botanic garden "in a fine
situation in the neighbourhood of Edinburgh". The land had been
purchased from the Rocheids of Inverleith and its fourteen and a
half acres form the basis of the modern Royal Botanic Garden.
According to Lord Cockburn the Rocheids were an enormously
proud family and it is fitting that their elegant house should
now house the Gallery of Modern Art within the gardens. The
gardens today occupy some seventy-five acres and are notable
for the rhododendrons, rock garden, and elegant greenhouses.

# February

*The Royal Mile is the main thoroughfare of the original old town of Edinburgh
and it runs like a spine down the ridge of the Castle rock to the Palace of
Holyroodhouse. Many of the city's oldest buildings, towering tenements, now
happily restored, line its cobbled length.*

# February

**1st** _____

**2nd** _____

**3rd** _____

# February

**1st**

**1811:** As the crew of the lightship *Pharos* extinguished its lights for the last time, a thin pencil of light shone eerily across the dark waters of the North Sea. The Bell Rock lighthouse, designed by Robert Stevenson, had sprung into life and a long chapter of shipwreck and tragedy on that isolated reef had come to an end. Robert was the first in a long line of Edinburgh engineers who strung a necklace of lighthouses around Scotland's rugged coastline from the Bell Rock to Skerryvore in the Hebrides. Their work continued into the twentieth century and the only Stevenson to have made a name for himself in other fields was Robert's grandson, the novelist Robert Louis Stevenson. The Northern Lighthouse Board has its headquarters in George Street and its supply ship is still called *Pharos*.

**2nd**

**1891:** The managers of the Royal Infirmary finally agreed to admit women as medical students and allowed them to be taught in separate classes unless the lecturers themselves favoured mixed groups of students. Following the efforts of the remarkable Sophia Jex-Blake and Elizabeth Garrett twenty years earlier to break down the male bastions of medical power and privilege within its medical faculty, the University of Edinburgh and the Infirmary had agreed to admit women students in 1872 but in conditions that were extremely inconducive to proper study. They were not allowed to attend post mortems or major operations and were only allowed in certain wards at set times, hardly the best means of securing a proper medical education. The last restrictions were not removed until 1927.

**3rd**

**1851:** The foundation was laid for the building in West Coates near Haymarket which was to become Donaldson's School. Built at a cost of £100,000 which had been left in the bequest of James Donaldson, it specialised — and still does — in the teaching of deaf children. One of the most imposing buildings in Edinburgh, the school stands in its own ample grounds and it was designed in an ornate Tudor Jacobean style by the distinguished architect W. H. Playfair. The elegant frontage is crowned by a four-storey tower with four octagonal turrets and there are three-storey towers at each corner of the quadrangular building. Legend has it that Queen Victoria demanded that the building be used as the Royal residence in Edinburgh in preference to Holyroodhouse.

# February

4th _____

5th _____

6th _____

# February

## 4th

**1818:** The Royal regalia of Scotland which had been missing since the passing of the Act of Union in 1707 were discovered at a carefully stage-managed ceremony within the Castle. At the persuasion of Sir Walter Scott, the government had set up a commission to seek out Scotland's "Honours" — the crown, sceptre and sword of state — and they were eventually discovered in a state of perfect preservation in a long, oblong oaken chest in a room in the Castle. The discovery was hailed by the raising of the Royal Standard and by the firing of a salute from the Castle's guns. Scott, who was present at the time of the opening of the chest, is said by his biographer, John Gibson Lockhart, to have been moved by "the deepest emotion". The regalia are today on display in the Castle.

## 5th

**1881:** The historian and philosopher Thomas Carlyle died at his house in Cheyne Walk, Chelsea, in London. Although he came from Ecclefechan in Dumfriesshire, Carlyle had enjoyed long and close links with Edinburgh. He was a student at the University between 1809 and 1813 and after a period school teaching in Kirkcaldy in Fife he returned to live in the city from 1818 until 1828 when he and his wife, Jane Welsh, lived in Comely Bank. During that period he became a close friend of Francis Jeffrey, the editor of the *Edinburgh Review*, and he also spent much of his time translating Goethe. In 1866 Carlyle had been elected Lord Rector of the University, an honour he much treasured, and at his inauguration — which was held in the Music Hall in George Street— he spoke of his debt to "a life full of reading".

## 6th

**1787:** During his stay in Edinburgh, Robert Burns petitioned the bailies of the Canongate for permission to raise a stone over the unmarked grave of Robert Fergusson in the Canongate churchyard. Burns had been influenced at an early stage by Fergusson and wished to raise "some memorial to direct the steps of the lovers of Scottish song, when they wish to shed a tear over the 'narrow house' of the bard who is no more, is surely a tribute due to Fergusson's memory — a tribute I wish to have the honour of paying." The inscription is:

> *No sculptured marble here, nor pompous lay,*
> *No storied urn nor animated bust;*
> *This simple stone directs Pale Scotia's way*
> *To pour her sorrows o'er her poet's dust.*

# February

7th _____

8th _____

9th _____

# February
## 7th

**1858:** Dr Henry Littlejohn, the pioneer of public health work, called at the house of John Gray in Hall Court in the Cowgate and secretly diagnosed what he had long feared, that his patient had tuberculosis. Three days later Gray, a policeman in the Edinburgh City and County Police Force, died and was buried in Greyfriars churchyard. After his death, workers in the cemetery began to notice that Gray's dog, a Skye terrier called Bobby, had taken up vigil on his master's grave and refused to be moved. Gradually residents in the area of Candlemaker's Row fed and cared for the dog and he became something of a pet and a curiosity for visitors. He acquired a nickname — Greyfriars Bobby — and in 1867 the Lord Provost, William Chambers, arranged for his licence to be paid by the city. Greyfriars Bobby died in 1872.

## 8th

**1599:** The death occurred of Robert Rollock, the first principal of the "Tounis College" or as it came to be known, the University of Edinburgh. A divine schooled in philosophy and theology, Rollock was an outspoken commentator on religious matters and a firm supporter of the Reformed Church in Scotland, but today he is best remembered for laying the foundations of the fledgling university. David Masson, a nineteenth-century Professor of English, would begin each academic session with a lecture extolling Rollock's virtues and his importance to Scottish academic history. He was, said Masson, "the first president of one of the most important institutions in the Scottish nation". With Rollock as its head, the University was first housed near the church of St Mary in the Field.

## 9th

**1831:** One of Edinburgh's most popular ministers, Andrew Thomson, who had charge of the noble St George's Church in Charlotte Square, died and was buried in the churchyard of St Cuthbert's. He was the first minister of a church that had excited considerable controversy within the city. Its massive bulk occupied the western side of a square that in Craig's original plan for the New Town was to have been matched by another church in St Andrew Square, but the symmetry was spoiled by the earlier construction of a town house in the latter square. St George's was designed by Robert Reid and built at a cost of £33,000, opening in 1814. The design is a scaled-down version of St Paul's in London, and today it houses the annexe of the Public Record Office and is known as West Register House.

# February

10th _____

11th _____

12th _____

# February

## 10th

**1567:** Nine days after he had taken up residence in the house of Kirk o' Field — a small, domestic house in the quadrangle of the Collegiate Church of St Mary in the Field, now long lost beneath the massive pile of the Old College on South Bridge — Henry, Lord Darnley, husband to Mary Queen of Scots, woke early to the sounds of hurried activity in the grounds of the house he thought to be secure. There in the dark he would have seen the armed men of the powerful 4th Earl of Bothwell, making their final preparations for mining the house. With no time to dress, he fled the house clad only in his nightgown and cape, but escape was out of the question. With his servant, Darnley was quietly and efficiently strangled, minutes before the house erupted in a mighty explosion.

## 11th

**1936:** The House of Commons was informed that the ancient title of the office of Governor of Edinburgh Castle was to be revived and that the General Officer, Commanding-in-chief, Scottish Command, General Sir Archibald R. Cameron, would hold the post. The new holder of this honorary title, which had slipped into abeyance in 1860, could expect a somewhat quieter existence than many of his predecessors who were expected to defend the Castle to the last man when it was under siege. Amongst the more famous Governors were Sir William Kirkcaldy of Grange who held it for Mary Queen of Scots, and the Duke of Gordon who eventually had to yield to the Orange forces after he had maintained with honour his allegiance to James VII and II. The Castle was last besieged during the Jacobite rebellion of 1745.

## 12th

**1829:** Outside the house of Dr Robert Knox at 4 Newington Road (now number 17) a large crowd gathered to demonstrate against Knox's part in the notorious Burke and Hare case. Two weeks previously William Burke had been hanged for his part in supplying corpses for Dr Knox's anatomy class, and although Edinburgh was well used to the activities of bodysnatchers or "resurrectionists" what had incensed the crowd was that Burke and Hare murdered to produce a good supply of bodies. Clearly most people felt that Knox had shut his eyes to the murders and the mob was intent on revenge. Windows were smashed, an effigy of the doctor was hanged and burned, and the City Guard had to be called to restore order. Knox was cleared of any crime but was forced ultimately to leave the city.

# February

13th ——————————————————————————

14th ——————————————————————————

15th ——————————————————————————

# February

## 13th

**1685:** Sir Robert Sibbald, Physician to the King and Geographer-Royal for Scotland, raised an action in the Court of Session against Lady Rosyth "for his damage incurred by the negligence of hir and hir servant woman, in burning his house in Edinburgh, in April last". A fine was imposed on Lady Rosyth but Sibbald, who held the public posts of Professor of Medicine in the University and the presidency of the Royal College of Physicians, was fast becoming unpopular in the city for his conversion to Catholicism. Later in the year a mob was to storm his house in Carrubber's Close and he only escaped assassination by fleeing to London. Before his death in 1722 Sibbald reverted to Protestantism since, as he admitted in his memoirs, he wanted nothing more than to "return to the Church I was born in".

## 14th

**1934:** The benefactor of St Peter's Roman Catholic Church, Marc André Raffalovitch, a Russian emigre, was found dead when the taxi that called to take him to daily Holy Communion arrived at his house at 9 Whitehouse Terrace. Built in 1907 on the Falcon estate in Morningside to a design by the distinguished architect Sir Robert Lorimer, St Peter's is one of the noblest churches in the city and is remarkable for its casual mixture of traditional Scottish lines with European influences never far away. The first priest was the remarkable Father John Gray, Raffalovitch's friend, who had pressed hard in Rome for the construction of the new church. Before his conversion to Catholicism in 1898 Gray had been a poet and critic in London and a friend of Oscar Wilde and Max Beerbohm.

## 15th

**1848:** The Caledonian Railway opened its first station in Edinburgh on a site in Lothian Road to inaugurate their train service to Glasgow in competition with the rival Edinburgh and Glasgow service that had been started six years earlier, and which was later taken over by the North British. The station remained in use until 1870 when it became a goods yard and the foundation stone was laid for the Caledonian Railway's Princes Street Station at the West End. However, financial difficulties beset its construction and it was not completed until 1903 when the Caledonian Hotel was opened on the same site. Princes Street Station served the old Caledonian routes to the west and south-west and after nationalisation it continued to offer through train services to the English Midlands. It was closed to traffic in 1965 and is now a car park.

# February

16th ——————————————————————————

17th ——————————————————————————

18th ——————————————————————————

# February

## 16th

**1705:** From his printing house at the foot of Horse Wynd in the Cowgate, Andrew Symson published his most elaborate work, TRIPATRIARCHICON; *or the Lives of the Three Patriarchs, Abraham, Isaac, and Jacob, extracted forth of the sacred story and digested into English.* Although this curious, yet ingenious, piece of poesy has long since disappeared into time's wastepaper basket, Symson deserves his place in Edinburgh's history as one of the printers who inherited the fine craftsmanship of the city's first printers, Chapman and Myllar, who had set up their press in 1507 during the reign of James IV. Symson was a man of great learning and was for a time amanuensis to the Lord Advocate, Sir George Mackenzie of Rosehaugh, the founding genius of the Advocates' Library.

## 17th

**1688:** During the "killing times", that grim period of the Covenanting opposition, about eighteen thousand Covenanters were killed, many of them executed in the Grassmarket in Edinburgh. One of the most notorious was the execution of James Renwick, a Cameronian field preacher who had been forced to live in Holland because of his beliefs and on his return was arrested and taken to Edinburgh. His death is commemorated in the Martyrs' Monument, an imposing structure in the Greyfriars churchyard. Its inscription reads: "From May 27th 1661, that the noble Marquis of Argyle was beheaded to the 17th February 1688 that Mr James Renwick suffered, were one way or other murdered and destroyed for the same cause about eighteen thousand of whom were executed at Edinburgh about one hundred. . . ."

## 18th

**1842:** The Edinburgh and Glasgow Railway Company, which had been formed in 1838, officially opened their fifty-six-mile railway route between Edinburgh and Glasgow via Carstairs in Lanarkshire. In 1845 the company was taken over by the Caledonian Railway and a new, shorter route via Midcalder opened in 1869 thus reducing the journey time between the two cities. Trains consisting of a total of fifty-two carriages carried the specially invited guests from Edinburgh to Glasgow where there was a civic banquet in honour of the occasion— although it will come as no surprise to those who complain about the present-day service to learn that the return journey was delayed by three-and-a-half hours due to vandalism on the line.

# February

19th _____

20th _____

21st _____

# February
## 19th

**1947:** A hundred squatters were evicted from derelict property in St John Street in the Canongate. They had taken refuge in a building that had been condemned by the Town Council as being unsafe and insanitary and the police were called in to effect their removal. Many of the families made last-minute arrangements to stay with relatives but some thirty people were made completely homeless by the action and they were removed to the Northern General Hospital where they were allowed to stay for a few days while alternative housing was found for them. Early the next day the sticks of furniture that could not be removed were cleared by the Cleansing Department and nothing remained of the squatters' vain attempt to stay in the street that had once been their home.

## 20th

**1934:** The Rev. Canon Thomas Hannan writing about ghosts in the Canongate reported in *The Scotsman:* "I saw my first shade in an old house in the Abbey Strand having walked down the street called Abbeyhill from Abbey Mount. Near the junction of Abbeyhill with the Canongate workmen were busy doing something to the wall of the house and to the footpath in front of it. After exchanging remarks with the men I swung round to the Strand to look at a fine old wall which faces the Palace: the ancient aspect of the wall has often attracted me. Next I mounted the stair which gives access from the Strand to the house on which the workmen were busy. I wanted to see the interior of some of the many homes into which the house is divided and I . . . raised my first ghost . . . it was a little one, that of a child. . . ."

## 21st

**1842:** Although many rail commuters may not realise it, the grimy structure of Haymarket station is a listed building and with its opening to the public it became the city's first principal railway station on the newly opened Edinburgh to Glasgow route. It is still an important secondary station serving the west of Edinburgh and in 1979 and 1980 its platform facilities were improved and upgraded. The neighbouring Haymarket marshalling yards serviced in steam days the crack locomotives that hauled the east coast expresses to London, and the present-day locomotive power units continue that tradition by coping with the needs of the fleet of British Rail diesel-powered locomotives. Until the closure in 1962 of the suburban railway, Haymarket was one of the principal stops.

# February

22nd _____

23rd _____

24th _____

# February

## 22nd

**1825:** For the second time within three months, the High Street was hit by a serious fire. Although it did not spread as quickly as the great fire of November 1824, the conflagration in Lady Lovat's House at the head of Blackfriars Wynd destroyed the upper flats of this six-storey tenement and only prompt action by the firemen prevented a greater tragedy. After the previous fire the Town Council had introduced regulations for the newly formed department but these had been much criticised for the formality of their instructions and their insistence on a proper etiquette for entering people's property. Nevertheless, they did speed up the arrival of the firemen and their engines at subsequent fires in the city, no doubt saving many of the old buildings in the High Street which were to be the targets of several disastrous fires as the century progressed.

## 23rd

**1827:** For much of his lifetime Sir Walter Scott refused to put his name to his highly successful novels and preferred to be known as "The Great Unknown", or, more simply, as "The Author of Waverley". There were several reasons for his love of anonymity: a belief that a respected lawyer should not be an author, his own love of mystery, and a personal feeling that the revelation of his identity would over-expose him. Although his identity as an author had long been an open secret in Edinburgh, Scott agreed to reveal himself at a theatrical fund dinner in the Assembly Rooms, George Street, after Lord Meadowbank acknowledged Scott as the author of the Waverley novels to a large and enthusiastic audience who, according to one witness, climbed on to tables and chairs to add to their ringing applause.

## 24th

**1749:** According to the protocol book of William Forbes, a burgess who kept a close record of the names of the city's streets and closes, Anchor Close, off the High Street, was once known as Forglen's or Forgulan's Land from the ownership of Sir Alexander Ogilvie of Forglen. An earlier name was Fowler's Close because it contained the house of William Fowler, a burgess and a poet who lived there in the sixteenth century but it took its present name from the Anchor Tavern, the drouthy home of the drinking club, the Crochallan Fencibles. One of the club's most famous members was the printer William Smellie, the printer of, and the main contributor to, the first *Enyclopaedia Britannica*. When Burns visited Edinburgh in 1786, Smellie quickly introduced him to the delights of the Anchor Tavern.

# February

25th _____

26th _____

27th _____

# February

25th _____

**1862:** The creator of the highly successful, though subsequently controversial, children's book, *The Story of Little Black Sambo*, Helen Bannerman, was born in a house at 35 Royal Terrace, the daughter of a minister of the Free Church of Scotland. Part of her childhood was spent in Madeira and she was educated privately in Edinburgh. Her family's financial difficulties forced her to work as a governess but she still found the time to work for an external degree at the University of St Andrews. Following her marriage to Dr Will Bannerman in 1889 she lived in India until her husband's retirement in 1918. It was from there that she began writing the illustrated letters to her children that culminated in the publication of *Little Black Sambo*, and a further nine books on similar themes.

26th _____

**1697:** There is a tradition in Edinburgh that the first causeway, or street, was laid by a Frenchman called Marlin. Many streets were laid with granite cobblestones, or setts, which came to be known as "causey-stanes". Their maintenance was obviously a matter of concern to the city fathers: "The contract between the Town and Robert Leitch, causeway layer of Glasgow is recorded. The latter is obliged to lay, repair and maintain all the causeways within the town, including the vennels and closes, and that part of the south side of the Canongate from St John's Cross which belongs to the royalty of the town; and also the causeways of all the entrances and avenues, ways and passages, leading to and from the same, and of that part of the town of Leith which the town of Edinburgh are in use to repair."

27th _____

**1414:** At the Tolbooth of Edinburgh Sir Robert Logan, lord of Restalrig, ratified his decision of 1398 to allow the city to enlarge the harbour which lay at the foot of the Water of Leith on the River Forth estuary and to allow a road to be built from the city through his property to the port. Restalrig is now a suburb of the city but it is notable for its ancient parish church and the adjoining fifteenth-century St Triduana's Aisle. The church stems from the same period and it was heavily restored by William Burn in 1836. With its heavy buttresses and intricate tracery, it is a handsome landmark in the style that has come to be known as Scots Gothic. A porch was added in 1886 and the modern vestry which stands on the site of the sacristy dates from 1962.

# February

28th _____

29th _____

# February

**28th** _____

**1638:** The document that has come to be known as the National Covenant was signed in the Greyfriars Church, first of all by the lairds opposed to King Charles I's ecclesiastical policies in Scotland. The following day it was signed by three hundred ministers and commissioners for the Scots burghs and in two further days of general enthusiasm and excitement the people of Edinburgh also trooped into the church to add their names to an historical document that set out the basic tenets of the Presbyterian Church of Scotland. One result of the signing of the Covenant was the spasmodic conflicts known as the Bishops' Wars, that broke out subsequently between the Covenanters and the Royalist forces of King Charles I.

**29th** _____

**1980:**
> *Now morn, with bonny purpie-smiles,*
> *Kisses the air-cok o' St Giles;*
> *Rakin their ein, the servant lasses*
> *Early begin their lies and clashes;*
> *Ilk tells her friend of saddest distress,*
> *That still she brooks frae scouling mistress;*
> *And wi' her joe in turnpike stair*
> *She'd rather snuff the stinking air,*
> *As be subjected to her tongue,*
> *When justly censur'd in the wrong.*

The air–cock, the weather vane on the steeple of St Giles, a well-known landmark celebrated in Robert Fergusson's poem *Auld Reekie*, was taken down for regilding following damage in a storm.

# March

The Royal Botanic Gardens at Inverleith contain over 35,000 species of plants and the gardens are memorable for the early flowering banks of rhododendrons, a lavish rock garden and the spectacular architecture of the greenhouses. The gardens also house the Gallery of Modern Art.

# March

1st _____

2nd _____

3rd _____

# March

## 1st

**1883:** In front of a large invited company the Lord Provost, Sir George Harrison, unveiled Sir John Steell's statue of Alexander and Bucephalus which was intended to stand on the west side of St Andrew Square at the intersection with George Street. Modelled as long ago as 1832, when the maquette attracted a good deal of comment from his peers, the work is generally considered to be the most accomplished piece of this prolific Edinburgh sculptor. In his own words, the statue was supposed to reflect "the predominance of the mind over brute force" and a contemporary critic, Sir John McNeill, said of it that "if a school of sculpture has been erected in Scotland we owe it to Steell . . .". Today the statue adorns the forecourt of the City Chambers in the High Street.

## 2nd

**1614:** The charter for St James Chapel in Newhaven was signed at Whitehall by King James I of Great Britain thus bringing an end to arguments that had raged for several years over the ownership of the feus from the chapel's lands. Founded in 1506 to provide for the spiritual welfare of shipwrights and mariners associated with the harbour, the St James Chapel had a comparatively brief existence and was dissolved at the time of the Reformation. Thereafter, the grounds were used as a burial ground for "Our Lady's Port of Grace", the other name by which the port of Newhaven was known, and the tithes of the chapel passed to the Kirk Session of Leith in name and on behalf of the poor of that burgh. Although the chapel disappeared, the revenue continued as feu duties from the houses built on the site.

## 3rd

**1819:** A meeting of noblemen and gentlemen under the chairmanship of the Duke of Atholl decided to promote the construction of a National Monument on Calton Hill to commemorate victory in the recently completed Napoleonic Wars. It was agreed that the monument should incorporate a church and that it should be an exact replica of the Parthenon in Athens. The architect was William Playfair, who also designed the neighbouring observatory, and although the foundation stone was laid in 1822 during George IV's visit to Edinburgh, the necessary finance had been exhausted by 1830 and all that remains of the project is twelve pillars of Craigleith sandstone. Over the years it has become a memorial to its own extravagance and it is popularly known as "Scotland's Disgrace".

# March

4th _____

5th _____

6th _____

# March

## 4th

**1890:** The Forth Railway Bridge, a wonder of Victorian engineering that seems to have been built from a child's Meccano set, was opened officially by the Prince of Wales, later King Edward VII. With its intricate patterns of tubular steel girders and trellis-work it carries the main railway line to Fife and the north and so massive is its structure that no sooner have the resident painters finished its annual repainting than they have to start all over again. Prior to its opening, trains had to be transferred across the River Forth by train ferries from Granton, but the siting of the bridge over the River Forth at Queensferry harks back to the ancient right of the burgh to ferry passengers across the river granted to them in 1130 by the Royal Charter of King David I.

## 5th

**1690:** In an act of unprecedented levity, the Town Council decided to postpone its meeting "till Wednesday next in respect the race is to be at Leith upon Friday". Horse races were an important part of the Edinburgh social calendar and the main meeting was held on Leith Links before moving to its present site at Musselburgh. The Council themselves awarded an annual silver cup and as Robert Fergusson observed a century later, going to the races was a time of fun for all even though it meant that some returned home penniless!

> *The races o'er, they hale the dools,*
> *W' drink o' a' kin-kind;*
> *Great feck gae hirpling hame like fools,*
> *The cripple lead the blind.*

## 6th

**1947:** The Lord Provost, Sir John Falconer, announced that a fragment of the Castle rock suitably encased in a solid silver setting would be presented to the city of Dunedin in New Zealand. The reliquary was the design of Pilkington Jackson who had picked up the rock fragment when masons were preparing the top of the Castle rock to take the Altar Stone that carries the Casket of Remembrance in the National War Memorial. One side of the rock was polished and the other left with tool marks, and it was set in a silver mounting bearing the coats of arms of both cities. The first mention of Edinburgh is in Ptolemy's *Geography* of around AD 160 where a race of people, the Votadini or Goddodin, gave the town its first name of Dunedin, meaning the fortress on the hill, the derivation of the present name.

# March

7th ————————————————————————————

8th ————————————————————————————

9th ————————————————————————————

# March

## 7th

**1744:** The Town Council awarded a Silver Club to be played for annually by "several Gentlemen of Honour skillful in the ancient and healthful exercise of the golf". Those gentlemen had met previously in a pub in Leith under the presidency of Duncan Forbes of Culloden and they formed the nucleus of the club that was to become the Honourable Company of Edinburgh Golfers. It now has its headquarters at Muirfield in neighbouring East Lothian. They laid down the original rules of the game of golf (now presided over by the Royal and Ancient club in St Andrews) and the Company introduced the two-ball foursome game, known the world over as the "Scotch Foursome". At their Muirfield course the Honourable Company has staged many of the world's leading competitions.

## 8th

**1962:** One of Edinburgh's most popular Lord Provosts of recent times, Sir Will Y. Darling, made his native city a bequest of £2,500 to endow a prize in his name for good citizenship. The purpose of the award, which was to be made annually, would be to recognise a citizen who had done most to promote Edinburgh's honour or welfare. Darling was a noted Edinburgh businessman who owned an elegant Princes Street store which carried his name and which was to disappear during the redevelopments of the nineteen-seventies. He also had an interest in the Edinburgh Bookshop in George Street and wrote two amusing books about the bookselling trade: *Private Papers of a Bankrupt Bookseller* and *Bankrupt Bookseller Speaks Again*. For a time he was M.P. for South Edinburgh.

## 9th

**1566:** While Mary Queen of Scots was dining alone with her entourage, her husband, Lord Darnley, entered her rooms in Holyroodhouse. He was followed by the ghastly spectre of the dying Lord Ruthven dressed in full armour beneath his dirty nightgown. Other conspirators followed with murder in their hearts. Their target was David Rizzio, Mary's secretary and something of a favourite and confidante at court. Despite his multi-lingual terror, "Justizia! Justizia! Madame! Save ma vie, save ma vie!", the pregnant Queen was powerless to help, being held at pistol point, and Rizzio was savagely cut to death in front of her eyes by the conspirators who took care to implicate the wretched Darnley. Rizzio's blood is still supposed to stain the floor in the apartment at Holyroodhouse.

# March

10th _____

11th _____

12th _____

# March

## 10th

**1863:** As a mark of recognition for their services to the youth of the city, the "Water Rats" of the philanthropist John Hope were permitted to take part in the ceremonies in Edinburgh to mark the marriage of the Prince of Wales. The "Water Rats" were precursors of the Boy Scouts or the Boys' Brigade and they had been established in 1860 to offer marching, drilling and band practice for boys over "4 feet 6 inches". Their drill hall was in Rose Street behind the Music Hall and their instructors were ex-army sergeants. On several occasions the boys acted as guard of honour at Holyroodhouse but there was also a para-military aspect to their training and they took part in several military exercises in the Queen's Park where they were known as the "Wee Warriors" by the participating soldiers.

## 11th

**1889:** In the early dawn of a frosty spring morning Jessie King, the Stockbridge "baby farmer", walked the short distance across the yard of Calton Jail to the execution chamber where she was hanged for the murder of three illegitimate children who had been placed in her care. Jessie King, a sad, dishonest, weak woman who had a tendency to drink heavily, had been sentenced to death largely on the evidence of her lover, Pearson, or Macpherson as he was better known. Although there was a good deal of revulsion about the murders of the children, there was also a strong feeling within the city that Jessie King was too piteous a case to face the gallows and a petition had been drawn up, unsuccessfully as it turned out, to win her a reprieve.

## 12th

**1656:** Following years of exhorting the citizens of Edinburgh to keep the streets clear of household rubbish and farmyard animals, the city fathers appointed two deacons whose task it was "to lay doun a way for clenging of the Toun ather be scaffingerie or uther wayis be appoynting a man in everie quarter of the Toun with power to them to settle the same the best they can . . .". The appointment of the rubbish removers did little to ease the problem, and filth of every kind continued to be thrown, willy-nilly, into the streets, forcing a visitor to Edinburgh, Daniel Defoe, to remark that the city's inhabitants "delighted in Stench and Nastiness". It was only during the nineteen-seventies that Edinburgh built a modern sewage disposal system in Leith for the Forth estuary.

# March

13th ———————————————————————————

14th ———————————————————————————

15th ———————————————————————————

# March

## 13th

**1812:** At a packed house in the Theatre Royal in Shakespeare Square (on which site at the east end of Princes Street the present General Post Office now stands), the famous actress, Sarah Siddons, made her farewell performance in Edinburgh in a production of *Henry the VIII*. She had been a popular dramatic visitor to the city for some thirty years and one of the great moments in Scottish theatrical history had been her first night in Edinburgh in 1784 when she had electrified the audience with her performance as Belvidera in Thomas Otway's *Venice Preserved*. Her farewell, at the age of fifty-seven, was marked by a cheering audience so tightly crowded into the theatre that a contemporary witness remarked that many lost their coats and hats in the crush.

## 14th

**1312:** During his campaign against King Edward II of England, every castle in Scotland had fallen to King Robert the Bruce except Edinburgh which was held by Sir Pier de Lombard. The English, however, suspected their commander of treason (rightly as it turned out) and imprisoned him. During the subsequent confusion, a Scottish raiding party under Thomas Randolph, Earl of Moray, stormed the Castle by the ingenious method of making a night-time ascent of the northern edge of the Castle rock that overhangs Princes Street Gardens. That they were successful owed much to the sure-footed guidance of William Frank, a soldier in the Scottish ranks, who had previously used the same route to visit his girl-friend. During excavations in 1821 traces were found of steps cut into the rock along the route taken by Moray and his thirty men.

## 15th

**1689:** The day after he had entered into discussion with the Scottish parliament, the Duke of Gordon, who was holding Edinburgh Castle for the deposed King James VII and II, replied that he would consider its surrender provided that certain conditions could be met concerning the safety of his garrison. Following sporadic exchanges of gunfire between the garrison and the besieging troops, Gordon continued the dialogue but it was not until the middle of June that the final surrender was made. During this period the most notable event was the scaling of the Castle rock by Graham of Claverhouse, the Jacobite "Bonny Dundee", who tried, vainly as it turned out, to enlist Gordon's help in his struggle against the Orange forces. Claverhouse was killed at the Battle of Killiecrankie on 27th July.

*Newhaven Harbour*

# March

16th _____

17th _____

18th _____

# March

## 16th

**1561:** Nine months after her death the body of Mary of Guise, the widow of King James V and the Queen-Regent of Scotland, was taken under cover of night from the chapel of St Margaret to the port of Leith and shipped to France where it was buried at Rheims in the nunnery of St Peter, of which her sister was abbess. During the throes of the Reformation struggle in Edinburgh the previous year, Mary had been forced to take refuge in the Castle as English forces began to help the cause of the Reformers. There she became ill and her condition seemed almost to match that of the strife-torn country. When she died her body was placed in a lead coffin until it was safe to return her mortal remains to the country of her birth. Her death also saw the final removal of the French garrison from Leith.

## 17th

**1687:** Sir John Lauder, Lord Fountainhall, a judge of the Court of Session, gained a place in history not so much for the impartiality of his pleading as an advocate but rather for his wry diary, the *Historical Notices of Scottish Affairs*. In it he recorded the civic events of his time but he was not above minuting the detritus of everday life: "Captain Scot, in the King's life-guard, having lost his dog in the Colledge of Edinburgh, beats Mr Gregory Professor of Mathematicks, by mistake, thinking he had tane his dog. The University in a body having complained to my Lord Leviston, Captain, and my Lord Chancellor of this, as ane affront done to them, he was secured and put to crave pardon." It was around this time that the University began to assert its independence from the Town Council.

## 18th

**1663:** Since the beginnings of recorded civic history, Edinburgh has been bothered by outbursts of prostitution within the city's walls. Town Council edicts have thundered against fornicators and the keepers of bawdy-houses and, as startled citizens were surprised to discover, have continued to do so until the present day — a well-known New Town brothel closed spectacularly in the nineteen-seventies when the lively ladies staged a sit-in after their madame died. That it was nothing new can be seen in this edict of 1663. "Manie odious complaints being made that a great manie burgessis and indwelleris within the burgh keepe base baudie houssis and ressetes and interteins thairin all sort of vitious and scandalous personis . . . recommendid to the baillies furthwith to make tryall of all personis. . . ."

# March

19th _____

20th _____

21st _____

# March

## 19th

**1953:** The Canongate Burgh Cross, which is considered by many historians to be Edinburgh's oldest public monument, was removed from its site outside the Canongate Church to a garden which had been laid out on the site of the old church hall. The cross was first mentioned in the records of the city in the sixteenth century when it was said to stand in the middle of the street, on the "croon o' the causey", with a pillory or rack-stool beneath it and with the jougs on the shaft. Gradually the stonework of the cross began to deteriorate and in 1888 the shaft was provided with a new base. In its new site it is surrounded by paving stones and cast-iron railings incorporating the coat of arms of the old burgh of the Canongate — a stag's head with a cross in the antlers.

## 20th

**1963:** To mark the 150th anniversary of the birth of the Scottish explorer and missionary David Livingstone, a wreath was laid at his monument in Princes Street Gardens and the ceremony was followed by a service of thanksgiving in the High Church of St Giles. Among the descendants of Livingstone at the ceremonies were his grand-daughter, great-grandson and great-grand-daughter, and in his speech of welcome, Lord Provost Sir John Greig Dunbar recalled to them that David Livingstone had been made a freeman of the city in 1857. Livingstone, though, did not belong to Edinburgh — he was born in Blantyre in Lanarkshire, and after qualifying as a medical missionary he spent fifteen years in Southern Africa, becoming later a distinguished explorer and philanthropist.

## 21st

**1855:** The death occurred of Andrew Melrose, the part-owner of the famous firm of tea-brokers in Leith that bore his name. For the wholesale tea dealer the abolition in 1833 of the monopoly held by the East India Company had presented abundant opportunities for trade with India and China, and Andrew Melrose had set up his shop in the Canongate that same year. With a group of seven other merchants he organised the first shipment of tea to Leith when their chartered ship, the *Isabella*, returned in April 1835 with a cargo of seven thousand cases of the best China tea. Later, Andrew's son, William, joined him in the enterprise and that move allowed him to travel to China and to build up an unrivalled set of business contacts. For a time Melrose's was one of the leading Princes Street stores.

# March

22nd _____

23rd _____

24th _____

# March

## 22nd

**1859:** The National Gallery of Scotland, which nestles beneath the Mound, opened its doors to the public two years after the death of its designer, William Playfair. It houses the nation's collection of paintings and sculpture and in addition to its excellent Scottish collection, Rembrandt, Velazquez, El Greco, Van Dyck, Goya, Gaugain and Monet are amongst the many European painters represented in its permanent holding. Additional, modern galleries were opened in 1979 and one of the Gallery's delights is its collection of Turner watercolours from the Vaughan Bequest which are shown each January when they are least affected by the weak winter sun. The Royal Scottish Academy, facing on to Princes Street, is also by Playfair, whose name has been commemorated in the nearby steps up the Mound.

## 23rd

**1497:** Although it now largely runs beneath the suburb of Morningside, the Jordan Burn is one of the city's most ancient streams. The first recorded reference to it is from the protocol book of one James Young, a fifteenth-century burgess who recorded the principal events of his day and who referred to this pleasant stream by its alternative name of Pow Burn, "pow" being of Scandinavian derivation and meaning "pool" or "sluggish stream". The burn becomes the Jordan as it meanders through Morningside's so-called "Biblical Area" with its plethora of Old Testament street names. The burn's origins are clouded in mystery although several attempts have been made to trace its source and the line of its various tributaries. It flows into the sea at Portobello where it is the Figgate Burn.

## 24th

**1618:** The Fellowship and Society of Brewers of Ale in Edinburgh, which had been founded in 1598, agreed that the society should be dissolved and their lands on Bruntsfield sold to the Town Council for the common good. Beer had been brewed originally in Edinburgh by the monks of the Greyfriars and Blackfriars orders — and in the Canongate by the monks of the Abbey of Holyrood — and the society had been founded as a public company by the Town Council with the intention both of providing good cheap beer for Edinburgh's citizens and of developing the land around the Burgh Loch. The first intention was quickly stilled when people began to complain that the beer was expensive and, more to the point, weak, but the society did lay water pipes from the loch into the city.

# March

25th _____

26th _____

27th _____

# March

**25th** _____

**1617:** The Cross, a handsome structure which was the focal point of Edinburgh civic life, was re-erected in the High Street near St Giles. According to Chambers' *Traditions of Edinburgh*, it was "the rallying point of a species of lazzaroni called *Caddies* or *Cawdies* which formerly existed in Edinburgh, employing themselves chiefly as street-messengers and *valets de place*. A ragged, half-blackguard looking set they were, but allowed to be amazingly acute and intelligent, and also faithful to any duty entrusted to them. A stranger coming to reside temporarily in Edinburgh got a caddy attached to his service to conduct him from one part of town to another, to run errands for him; in short, to be wholly at his bidding. A caddy *did* literally know everything — of Edinburgh. . . ."

**26th** _____

**1603:** In the late evening a lone, exhausted horseman arrived at the gates of Holyroodhouse and demanded immediate entry. he was Sir Robert Carey, the brother of the English Lord Hunsdoun, who had ridden non-stop from London for two days to deliver important news to King James VI. His horse, the last he had been on, was led away foaming and on the point of collapse, and the weary Carey was ushered into the presence of the awakened King. Throwing himself onto his knees in front of his half-dressed Majesty, he uttered the words that James had been waiting so long to hear: "Queen Elizabeth is dead, Your Majesty is King of England." King James VI of Scotland had become King James I of England and the Union of the Crowns of Scotland and England had come into being.

**27th** _____

**1957:** Five months after a disastrous fire gutted their premises in Princes Street, the international clothing firm of C&A Modes floated into further difficulties when it was discovered that work on their new store had to be held up because one of Edinburgh's long-hidden subterranean streams had decided to resurface in the foundations. The stream had to be diverted before work could continue but in spite of that unexpected snag the shop was able to open on two floors by the end of the month and the upper floors were opened on schedule later in the year. By adopting new open-plan methods of shop presentation, C&A's were able to add up to one thousand feet of additional floor space. Sensibly, the Council's Planning Committee refused to sanction the use of advertising banners on the shop's facade.

# March

28th _____

29th _____

30th _____

# March

## 28th

**1666:** The Town Council noted that an additional gift of books worth "twa hundreth fourtie two pounds sixteen shilling" had been bestowed on the University library and "appoynts the saids buiks to be addit to the catalogues of the Librarie as all uther buiks ather bought or gifted thereto". The library owed its existence to a gift of three hundred books made by Clement Little to the first principal, Robert Rollock, shortly after the college's foundation in the late sixteenth century. Today the University library is one of the largest research libraries in the country, a reputation it enjoyed from its beginnings, as the Rev. Thomas Morer, an English visitor, testified: ". . . well furnish'd with books, and those put in very good order, and cloister'd with Doors made of Wire . . .".

## 29th

**1728:** Musical concerts were popular events in Edinburgh throughout the eighteenth century, especially in St Cecilia's Hall and Corri's Concert Rooms in Broughton Street. A music society was established by "a number of lovers of harmony" who resolved to meet weekly "for our mutual diversion and entertainment" with the object of performing "concerts of music as we have already done for these twelve months past". In his *History of Edinburgh* Maitland wrote that "the Society was so highly approved of that many persons of disinction applied to be admitted members . . . a few years after the erection of the Society, thirty persons were admitted, whereby the members were increased to one hundred in number who . . . divert themselves and friends in the most agreeable and delightful manner".

## 30th

**1625:** For two long days a fierce storm had raged along the whole of the east coast of Scotland, whipping up the waters of the North Sea and doing immense damage to ships in harbour and to surrounding property. The water in the harbour of Leith had risen to a previously unheard of height and many ships were destroyed, being dashed against each other and smashed on the piers. There was also considerable loss of life among the sailors who tried to make fast their ships during the night. It was to be several days before the full extent of the damage was known. The more superstitious began to fear that the storm was a harbinger of of national misfortune and their forebodings seemed to have some foundation when word reached Edinburgh that James VI and I had died on the 27th.

# March

31st_____

**1880:** William Gladstone, the leader of the Liberal Party, arrived in Edinburgh to conduct his parliamentary campaign for the seat of Midlothian—which was to be known thereafter as the Midlothian Campaign. Between 1868 and 1880 British politics had been dominated by the very different leaderships of Gladstone and his Tory rival, Benjamin Disraeli. Gladstone's thrust against the Tories in the 1880 General Election was the bankruptcy of their foreign policy, especially in the Balkans, and he argued that Britain's aims should be tempered by morality and justice free from the taint of self-interest. His powerful rhetoric attracted large crowds, many of which had been enfranchised by the 1867 Reform Act and the Midlothian Campaign (which Gladstone won) was one of the first to use modern popular electoral campaign methods.

# April

The Georgian New Town of Edinburgh, built in the latter half of the eighteenth century, is a miracle of town planning. With its broad symmetrical streets and plain, yet elegant, architecture blessed by the Smile of Reason, the new town offered a fresh alternative to the narrow confines of the medieval city.

# April

1st _____

2nd _____

3rd _____

# April

## 1st

**81:** On the slopes of the hill that bears his name in the centre of Edinburgh, Arthur, son of Uther Pendragon and Ygaerne, ventured forth with the knights of the round table to meet in battle the dog-faced warriors of the Hybee tribe whose land lay to the north near present-day Easter Road. So all day long the noise of battle rolled among the mountains by the winter sea until King Arthur's table, man by man, had fallen in Lyonnes about their Lord, King Arthur. The defeat was a sore loss to the knights of the round table who had been wont to meet in Duddingston where now stands the Sheep Heid Inn, but Arthur had made a pact with the world of faery and he and his men were whisked off to Avalon, which is thought to be in the neighbourhood of Portobello. All that remains of the day is Arthur's Seat, the site of his throne.

## 2nd

**1656:** The Town Council ordered two baillies to cross the Forth to Falkland in Fife to inspect the timber that had been recently felled and, if it was in good condition, to make arrangements for bringing it to Edinburgh, "for repaireing the herbour of Leith". Since the earliest days of Edinburgh's development as a city, Leith had been recognised as its harbour and, indeed, Robert the Bruce's charter of 1329 makes specific mention of Edinburgh's ownership of its dock area. Jurisdiction of Leith remained a bone of contention between the two communities and it was not until the end of the eighteenth century that the harbour was widened and deepened and supplied with proper facilities. The main docks, Edinburgh, Imperial, Victoria, and Albert, were built between 1852 and 1881.

## 3rd

**1976:** The Edinburgh Wax Museum opened in New Assemblies Hall in New Assembly Close, off the High Street. The museum contains waxwork models of famous characters from Scotland's history as well as a section devoted to "never never land" and a thoroughly realistic chamber of horrors. The elegant Georgian building which houses the museum was built in 1766 to house the balls, or dancing assemblies, that were such an important part of Edinburgh's social life during the eighteenth century. It has also acted as a tavern, a masonic lodge, of which Sir Walter Scott was once a member, a branch of the Commercial Bank of Scotland and as the headquarters of the Royal Scottish Society for the Prevention of Cruelty to Children.

# April

4th _____

5th _____

6th _____

# April

## 4th

**1617:** The inventor of logarithms, John Napier, died at his remote house of Merchiston, a name enshrined in the city by the modern suburb to the south of Bruntsfield. Napier had led the life of a recluse for many years and with his jet-black cockerel, which was thought to be his familiar, he was feared by his neighbours as being a wizard and a dabbler in the black arts.. A skilled mathematician, Napier also invented an early rudimentary calculator made of metal plates and ivory rods, known as "Napier's Bones". He was also an agricultural improver who was an advocate of the use of fertilisers, and amongst his other inventions were plans for a series of fearsome instruments of war including a huge burning mirror, powerful artillery and tanks and submarines.

## 5th

**1957:** After twenty-one years on the site, the principal bus operators in the Lothians, the Scottish Motor Traction Company (S.M.T.) opened its new bus station in St Andrew Square. As the scale of their operations had increased, so also had the complaints of the travelling public who wanted something better than platforms open to the elements and without any amenities. The new bus station provided an up-to-date set of shelters and refreshment stalls, waiting rooms and, to begin with, four long platforms capable of taking the estimated 120 buses an hour. An exhibition of buses was held on the opening day and the station commenced operations the following day, using the gyratory one-way system that is now in use in St Andrew Square. The site was further developed in the nineteen-sixties.

## 6th

**1790:** In the suburb of Abbeyhill, through which runs the A1 main road to London, stands the house of Marionville, a three-storeyed Georgian pile which has the distinguishing feature of a bow-fronted dormer window in the roof. It was once the home of a fashionable Dumfriesshire family, the Macraes, whose son, Captain Macrae, was well known both for his extreme courtesy and also for his fiery temper. After an argument outside an Edinburgh theatre over the ownership of a sedan chair, during which Sir George Ramsay's servant was assaulted by Captain Macrae, a duel was fought on Musselburgh beach between the two gentlemen and Ramsay was mortally wounded. The uproar against Macrae was so great that he was forced to leave the city and settle in Paris where he ended his days thirty years later.

# April

7th _____

8th _____

9th _____

# April

## 7th

**1933:** *The Scotsman* reported that: "At a meeting of Edinburgh Town Council—Lord Provost W. J. Thomson in the Chair—Lord Dean of Guild Maclennan moved approval of the recommendations of the Streets and Building Committee regarding applications for licences for illuminated advertisements in the Princes Street area. The committee recommended against allowing flashing sky signs or any illuminated sky signs or advertisements in premises to the south of Princes Street, visible from Princes Street at a height greater than 20 feet from the pavement. Within 20 feet such signs or advertisements would be subject to approval as regards design and other particulars including the colour." The motion was passed and there was substantial satisfaction that Princes Street would not become a "vulgar illuminated harliquinade".

## 8th

**1773:** The first official minutes of the Society of Golfers resolved to lift the club out of its increasingly moribund state and to "admit and receive" new members. It is likely that the Society had been in existence since the early seventeen-sixties but it was not until 1929 that it became known by Royal charter as the Royal Burgess Golfing Society of Edinburgh. The Society today has its spacious course and headquarters in the suburb of Barnton but it has previously golfed over Bruntsfield Links and at Musselburgh. A feature of the early club was its congenial habit of holding meetings in various taverns in the city, a custom that was continued until the nineteenth century when its members met in the elegant surroundings of the Café Royal in West Register Street.

## 9th

**1670:** On an open piece of ground between Edinburgh and Leith, near the site of the present-day Picardy Place, Major Thomas Weir, the commander of the City Guard, was strangled and burned to death. This bizarre character had led a devout, blameless life until he was seventy, when he admitted to his astonished neighbours a life spent in crime, wizardry and incest with his sister Grizel. In a state of mental collapse she too confessed to commerce with the Devil and to other sorceries with her brother, the Wizard and his magical staff. Grizel was hanged the same day in the Grassmarket, casting off her clothes in shame, but her brother refused absolution, asking to die as a beast in the flames in which his stick was cast to twist and writhe as if it had a life of its own.

# April

10th _____

11th _____

12th _____

# April

## 10th

**1735:** One of the closes swallowed up by the construction of the Royal Exchange (now the City Chambers) in 1761 was Mary King's Close, a street that enjoyed a notorious reputation for its supernatural goings-on. Chambers, in his *Traditions of Edinburgh*, wrote about a house in the close being haunted by "the head as of a dead person, looking him straight in the face. There was nothing but a head, though that seemed to occupy the precise situation in regard to the floor which it might have done had it been supported by a body of the ordinary stature". Other apparitions included poltergeists and there was no little joy when the close was finally closed up. Part of the close still exists beneath the City Chambers and in the protocol book of George Home it is referred to as Brown's Close.

## 11th

**1895:** After years of failing to agree which should be the most effective form of lighting for Edinburgh's streets, an electric lighting system, installed at a cost of some £120,000, was switched on by the wife of Lord Provost Sir Andrew Macdonald. A gaslight company had been formed as early as 1817 but it was not until 1822 that fifty-three gaslights had taken over from the seventy-nine oil-burning lights in Princes Street. With their warm glow and reassuring hiss, the gaslights were lit up at dusk by "leeries", men with lighting sticks who have been immortalised in Robert Louis Stevenson's poem: "O Leerie, see a little child and nod to him tonight". Gradually the more efficient but less romantic electric lights took over from gas all over the city's streets.

## 12th

**1916:** The Scottish socialist John Maclean was sentenced to three years' penal servitude for his part in the Glasgow protest meetings during which he had preached a philosophy that embraced international socialism and an end to the war in Europe. Maclean's imprisonment was spent at the now dismantled Calton Jail in Edinburgh and later at Peterhead, and the term in prison did much to undermine his health. After the war he was released and he became Lenin's Bolshevik consul to Scotland after the success of the Russian revolution, but he was arrested again in 1918 for sedition. Sentenced to a five-year term in prison, Maclean made his famous declaration to the court: "I come here not as the accused but as the accuser of capitalism dripping with blood from head to foot." He died in 1923.

# April

13th _____

14th _____

15th _____

*Leith Docks*

# April

## 13th

**1948:** Edinburgh International House, which had been established two years previously to provide a focus and meeting place for visitors to the city, announced that in preparation for the second Edinburgh Festival it would be increasing its amenities and enrolling up to 6,500 temporary members. In its headquarters in Princes Street International House offered a more convenient, and in many people's eyes, more convivial ambience than the Festival Club and it attracted many poets and painters who used the facility "open to midnight" to good advantage. Also included in the House that summer was an exhibition of contemporary Scottish paintings, and during the Festival itself an ambitious programme of symposia and discussions was put on for visitors and Festival-goers.

## 14th

**1582:** The Royal Charter for the foundation of the "Tounis College" was granted by King James VI and work on the college, that was to become the University of Edinburgh officially in 1858, began in the following year. In the beginning the college was housed in the Kirk of Field and the first students had taken up residence by October 1584. The first principal was Robert Rollock who built up a staff of "regents" to teach the classics and theology, thus giving the college an early leaning towards speculative thinking in the Humanities. Rollock was greatly helped by Clement Little's gift of three hundred books which formed the basis of the college's library. During the eighteenth and nineteenth century the University moved into Old College and the developments around Chambers Street.

## 15th

**1723:** By a codicil to the will of the well-known Edinburgh merchant George Watson, a sum of £100,000 Scots was increased to £140,000 Scots to be employed by his trustees "to raise a new Hospital for entertaining and educating the male children and grandchildren of decayed merchants in Edinburgh, which Hospital is to be called in future generations George Watson's Hospital". Watson also left money for other schools in the city including Heriot's and the Merchant Maidens' Hospital. His life is a memorial to the hard-headed businessmen who emerged in Edinburgh after the Act of Union of 1707 and whose industry promoted the ideas for the construction of the New Town. George Watson's College, now situated in Colinton, is administered still by the Merchants' Company of Edinburgh.

*Canongate rooftops*

# April

16th _____

17th _____

18th _____

# April

## 16th

**1851:** The Chartulary of the Canongate refers to Fletcher's Lodging in the Canongate, a rambling eighteenth-century building, now demolished, which was the town house of Andrew Fletcher of Milton, the Lord Justice-Clerk and the nephew of the Scottish patriot Andrew Fletcher of Saltoun. The house was also known as Lord Milton's Lodging but it is best remembered as the Milton House which gave its name to the school which now stands in front of the original site. Milton House was later occupied by a Roman Catholic school, a school for the deaf and the dumb, and its final use was the headquarters of the Royal Maternity Hospital. Its neighbour, Dirleton House, was reconstructed in 1954 as a replica of a seventeenth-century town house and several inscribed stones were used in the construction.

## 17th

**1767:** The Town Council announced that a little-known architect, James Craig, had been awarded their prize for the best plan of a new town to be built on the northern side of the city. For centuries Edinburgh had perched on the long ridge of rock between the Castle and Holyroodhouse and in the early part of the eighteenth century there had been considerable agitation for the construction of a modern extension to the city. Craig's plan allowed for the laying out of three main streets — Princes Street, George Street and Queen Street — to be intersected by three smaller streets and bounded at each end by Charlotte Square and St Andrew Square. Their formal elegance and symmetry was matched by the grandeur of the architecture, particularly by the houses of Robert Adam.

## 18th

**1677:** The Town Council was pleased to note that swans had returned to the waters of the Nor' Loch after an absence of almost a hundred years. "The councill being informed that Baillie Drummond hes gifted to the toun four swans there which will be verry pleasant to be seine sweming in the loch. The councill for the better preservatione of the saids swanes does apoynt a proclamtion to pas throw the toun dischargeing any persone or persones to kill or shoot fright or any wayes disturb the said swans under the pain of ane hundred pounds attour such personall punishment be imprissonment and putting of the transgressours in the stocks as the magistrats shall think fit." Today there is a bird sanctuary at Duddingston Loch.

# April

19th _____

20th _____

21st _____

# April

## 19th

**1703:** The following advertisement appeared in the *Edinburgh Gazette:* "There is a Boarding-school to be set up in Blackfriars Wynd, in Robinson's Land, upon the west side of the wynd, near the middle thereof, in the first door of the stair leading to the said land, against the latter end of May, or first of June next, where young Ladies and Gentlewomen may have all sorts of breeding that is to be had in any part of Britain, and great care taken of their conversation." Schools were connected with Blackfriars Wynd until the middle of the nineteenth century by which time it had become one of the most notorious slums in Edinburgh. It had taken its name by being the entrance to the long-disappeared Blackfriars Monastery and it had also housed the Edinburgh palace of Cardinal Bethune of St Andrews.

## 20th

**1878:** At Powburn, the ground of the Third Edinburgh Rifle Volunteers, Edinburgh's two best known football teams, Hibernian and Heart of Midlothian, played out the fourth replay of the final of the Edinburgh Football Association Cup. The final had been held on 9th February and it had ended in a goalless draw, although Hibs, as they are better known, had a goal disallowed. Three replays followed during which no goals were scored, but the fifth game was an exciting affair. With only a few minutes to go the match was deadlocked with two goals each but after a goalmouth melee, Alexander of Hearts knocked in the winning goal. The game ended in a near riot between the opposing sets of supporters and the Hearts captain was pursued back to his home in Causewayside by furious Hibs fans.

## 21st

**1787:** With the support of the Earl of Glencairn and the Gentlemen of the Caledonian Hunt, the publisher William Creech produced a second collection of the poems of Robert Burns — a collection that is generally known as the "Edinburgh Edition". For this edition Burns was paid the sum of 100 guineas but Creech allowed himself the right of producing other editions without the need to pay further royalty fees. Although Burns's poems had been published the previous year in Kilmarnock by John Wilson, the Edinburgh Edition established Burns's reputation as a major poet. It was brought out in London by Cadell and Davies and pirated editions soon appeared in places as far away as Canada and the United States of America. During his stay in the city, Burns failed in his attempt to find a patron.

# April

22nd ⎯⎯⎯⎯⎯⎯⎯⎯⎯⎯⎯⎯⎯⎯⎯⎯⎯⎯⎯⎯

23rd ⎯⎯⎯⎯⎯⎯⎯⎯⎯⎯⎯⎯⎯⎯⎯⎯⎯⎯⎯⎯

24th ⎯⎯⎯⎯⎯⎯⎯⎯⎯⎯⎯⎯⎯⎯⎯⎯⎯⎯⎯⎯

# April

## 22nd

**1859:** "A heavy fall of snow last night. Today the snow melts before
the sun, but in the shade it is a strong frost. I don't recollect
of such another event for upwards of 30 years. In the preaching
week of 1826 or (18)27 more probably the latter, I was intending
to go to the country, but was prevented by a heavy snowstorm
which lasted for several days. I have seen showers of snow in May."
From the diary of James Laurie, a devoted servant of the city of
Edinburgh, who became Town Clerk in 1859, shortly before his
death, and who kept an intimate record of the minutiae of civic
life, a diary that was probably intended for the distraction of
close relatives. His entry about unseasonal wintry weather in
the middle of spring could well have been echoed by other diarists
over the centuries.

## 23rd

**1664:** In the dark and narrow passages of the Tolbooth conditions
for the prisoners were unhealthy, fetid and most unpleasant as
this typical entry in the Old Tolbooth Records makes perfectly
clear: "I William Tempell chirurgeon Burges in Edr being called to
sie the legs & feet of James Smart prissoner in the iron house of the
tolbuth, and lying in irons, after that I visited his legs and feet,
I fund vpon his left lege at the joynt of his anckell bone ane gangrain
insewing vpon the tarsses and (?) of the joynts lyk as vpon the ryt
lege and foote a swelling wt a great quaggallat bloode lying vpon
the tarsse and mitta tarsse, The wch I testyfie to be a veritie befor
thir Edward Hill clarke ther and Hendrie monteith day and deat
forsd." Poor Smart was forced to stay in prison although the irons
were removed temporarily.

## 24th

**1717:** Two years before it became known by its present name of
Lady Stair's Close, the burgess Adam Watt referred to it as Lady
Gray's Close in his protocol book. This no doubt derived from
the house at the foot of the close which was built by Sir William
Gray in 1622. The house passed into the hands of Elizabeth,
Countess Dowager of Stair, in 1719, and it is from her that the
name of both house and close is derived. Early historians tended
to believe that the progenitor of the name was her daughter-in-law,
Eleanor, the widow of the Viscount Primrose. The Earl of
Rosebery acquired the house in 1895 and presented it, after
restoration, to the city who now use it as a museum for the relics
of its leading writers, Sir Walter Scott, Robert Louis Stevenson
and Robert Burns.

# April

25th _____

26th _____

27th _____

# April

## 25th

**1690:** After their protestations of loyalty to the House of Orange in the days following the Glorious Revolution of 1688, the Scottish Parliament began its second sitting in Edinburgh. There were momentous tasks in hand. All "outed" ministers were restored to their charges, Presbyterian church government was brought back and all thirty-three chapters of the Knoxian Confession of Faith were reaffirmed. It was also in that parliament that an Act was passed preventing women from concealing their pregnancies because if the child was subsequently found to have died "the Mother shall be holden and reputed the Murtherer of her own child". That "Act anent Murthering of Children" was used as a device in Sir Walter Scott's great Edinburgh novel *The Heart of Midlothian* when Effie Deans was condemned.

## 26th

**1886:** Duncan Maclaren, who had been Lord Provost of Edinburgh between 1851 and 1854 and its Member of Parliament from 1865 to 1881, died in the city which had been his home since the age of eighteen. The son of a Dunbartonshire farmer, Maclaren had worked as a draper with a business in the High Street but gradually political affairs began to occupy his life and he became a member of the Town Council as early as 1834. With his friend James Grant, the historian who wrote the celebrated *Old and New Edinburgh*, Maclaren was a member of the Society for the Vindication of Scottish Rights which was an early forerunner of the nationalist movement in Scotland. A great supporter of his native country and a promoter of her best interests, Maclaren was known in Westminster as the "Member for Scotland".

## 27th

**1764:** An advertisement in the *Edinburgh Advertiser* announced: "As many people have got benefit from using of the water of St Bernard's Well in the neighbourhood of the city, there has been such demand for lodgings this season that there is not so much as one room to be had either at the Water of Leith or its neighbourhood." St Bernard's Well, once noted for its spa waters, stands by the Water of Leith in a pleasant walk between the Dean Village and the suburb of Stockbridge. The Temple to Hygeia was designed by Alexander Naysmith for Lord Gardenstone in 1789 but the well has been out of use since the middle of the twentieth century when it was discovered that the waters were being polluted by effluvia from the Water of Leith. Tradition claims that the "health" waters were disgusting to taste!

# April

28th _____

29th _____

30th _____

# April

## 28th

**1838:** *The Scotsman* announced that "Kennington and Jenner will open their new establishment . . . 47 Princes Street, corner of St David Street on Tuesday 1 May with every prevailing British and Parisian fashion in Silks, Shawls, Fancy Dresses, Ribbons, Lace, Hosiery. And every description of Linen, Drapery and Haberdashery". The firm of Jenners, as it came to be known, is still one of the great Princes Street stores and it moved into its present substantial building after a disastrous fire in November threatened the future of the store. Additions were made in 1903, 1922 and 1980 to the building which was designed in the style of the Bodleian Library in Oxford by W. Hamilton Beattie and by Charles Jenner who, unfortunately, did not live to see his masterpiece completed.

## 29th

**1937:** A meeting of the Edinburgh Public Health Committee considered the future of four historic buildings in the Canongate: Morocco Land, Shoemakers Land, Bible Land and the old building which stood adjacent to the Canongate Tolbooth. The whole area had been the subject of public debate because, although it represented some of the best of old Edinburgh architecture, the buildings had fallen into unhealthy disrepair and were considered by many to be risks to the city's well being. The arguments within the committee fell into two parts: those who wanted to preserve something of the traditional domestic architecture of the Canongate and those councillors who were in favour of demolition and progress, especially the widening of the street in that locality. Rebuilding took place eventually in 1957.

## 30th

**1717:** After he had been tried for the murder of two young children in his charge, Robert Irvine was hanged by the Baron of Broughton and his hands were hacked off with the knife with which he had committed the dreadful deed. Due to the vagaries of the folk tradition in Edinburgh, the murder became associated with Gabriel's Road, a short oblique passage behind Register House, roughly the site of the present-day lane that runs along side the Café Royal and Guildford Arms public houses. It led across the New Town to its exit at the ancient village of Silvermills, now swallowed up in Stockbridge. The road was supposed to be haunted by Irvine's ghost and by the wraiths of other unfortunate beings who had met their ends in this ancient long-forgotten road which disappeared when the New Town was built.

# May

The bulk of Arthur's Seat, the mountain within the city, is Edinburgh's most distinguishing landmark. One of a group of long-extinct volcanoes that formed the city's topography, Arthur's Seat stands in the park of Holyroodhouse and from its easily climbed summit are the best views of the city.

# May

1st _____

2nd _____

3rd _____

# May

1st _____

**1707:** On the day that the Act of Union, joining together the parliaments of England and Scotland, came into force, there is a tradition in Edinburgh that a disgruntled citizen broke into the Church of St Giles and played upon its bells the old Scots air, "How can I be sad on my wedding day?". The country's attitude to the Act was predictably ambivalent: some, including those politicians and lawyers who had benefitted materially from the drafting of the Bill, were happy to embrace unionism, others were to feel acutely the loss of Scotland's independence. Throughout the years that have followed the joining together of two very different countries, the hurt to Scottish pride was to be a source of much bitterness and the twentieth century has seen the formation of a Scottish National Party.

2nd _____

**1970:** Meadowbank Sports Centre, a twenty-five-acre complex of facilities for outdoor and indoor sports, was opened by His Royal Highness the Duke of Kent. The project had been approved in November 1967 and was completed by the spring of 1970 at a cost of £2.3 million, in time for the Commonwealth Games of that same year. The aim of the centre was to provide the most intensive possible use of the ground for a large variety of sports all the year round and the facilities include a stadium, practice grounds, areas for squash courts and five multi-purpose halls. The largest of these has seating for 900 people and the whole design has been integrated to create an ambience to suit participator and spectator alike. Meadowbank is also the home of the football team, Meadowbank Thistle.

3rd _____

**1931:** After years of using makeshift premises, the foundation stone of a new synagogue was laid in Salisbury Road by Viscount Bearsted. The first synagogue in Edinburgh opened in a lane behind Nicolson Street before removing to premises in Richmond Court and later to Bristo House in Park Place. Nearby, on the south side of Sciennes House Place, is the old Jewish burial ground which was reached from Causewayside by a close then known as Jews' Close. The cemetery has long since closed and the burial ground of the Edinburgh Hebrew community is in the cemetery at Piershill. In his *Historic South Edinburgh*, Charles J. Smith points out that "Newington is the district in which Edinburgh's Jewish community is strongest, its earliest members coming here from Germany and the Low Countries".

# May

4th _____

5th _____

6th _____

# May

## 4th

**1722:** One of the most notorious judges to have practised in Edinburgh's courts — Robert MacQueen, Lord Braxfield — was born in Lanark. He was educated at the University of Edinburgh and was called to the bar in 1744 where he rapidly gained for himself a reputation as an expert in Feudal Law. In 1776 he became a Lord of Session and was appointed Justice Clerk in 1788 and it was in that capacity that he presided at the trials of Thomas Muir and the other political martyrs in 1793. Braxfield quickly gained an unpleasant name for himself as a hectoring bully who browbeat prisoners and their counsel alike. He is best remembered for his insult to a prisoner whom he condemned to death with the words that he would be "nane the waur for a hangin'". Stevenson used him as a model for *Weir of Hermiston*.

## 5th

**1603:** One of the first acts undertaken by King James VI on succeeding to the English throne was to establish a series of postmasters between Edinburgh and Berwick to ensure a reliable Royal postal system between the two countries. The postmasters were to receive set allowances and fees for keeping reliable horses for the service of the post by day and night "as has been done in England for many years". The post offices were to be situated at the foot of the Canongate, Haddington and Cockburnspath but it soon became obvious that the tasks appointed to the postmasters were too onerous and that the system was open to abuse. Stricter regulations were brought into force in 1616 but the Royal postal system relying on horsemen came to an end in 1786 with the introduction of mail coaches between the two capitals.

## 6th

**1656:** In Dock Street, Leith, stands the only remaining fragment of Leith Citadel which was built by John Milne after the Town Council passed an act "to fortifie the Toun of Leith ather by mantelling it about with a strong wall and bulwarkis or to build a Cittiedaill in South or North Leith". The intention was to provide accommodation for Cromwell's troops as well as to fortify the vulnerable harbour and its hinterland. General Monck, the Lord General of the parliamentary army, supervised the planning of the fortification which cost the city five thousand pounds Scots. Behind the citadel stood (and still stands) the North Leith burial ground which has been in use as a cemetery since 1664. The citadel, which was a large fort 400 feet by 250 feet, was demolished after the Restoration.

# May

7th _____

8th _____

9th _____

# May

## 7th

**1743:** The following advertisement appeared in the *Caledonian Mercury:* "The New Mansion House of Braid, commonly called the Hermitage, among enclosures and planting, on the banks of a burn in the neighbourhood of Edinburgh and Goat Whey, consisting of 6 rooms and 4 fine closets with kitchens, cellars, stable, byre, chaise house, flower garden and park of about 4 acres are to be let and entered immediately at yearly rent of £18 stg. or less." Hermitage House and the pleasant wooded valley in which it lies owes much to its second owner Charles Gordon who took a great interest in the cultivation of the whole area. The walk through the valley is still one of the most pleasant in Edinburgh but Hermitage House's future is still undecided after structural faults were found in it.

## 8th

**1980:** Gladstone's Land, the restored six-storey tenement in the Royal Mile which is in the safe hands of the National Trust for Scotland, was declared open by the Earl of Crawford and Balcarres, chairman of the Historic Buildings Council for Scotland. The building, which dates from 1620 and stands on the north side of the Lawnmarket, belonged to an Edinburgh merchant called Thomas Gladstone and in its long history it has enjoyed mixed fortunes. In the earlier part of the twentieth century it had become a dilapidated slum and in 1934 it was due to be demolished. However, a generous gift put it in the hands of the Trust and careful restoration revealed a pillared arcade and traditional painted ceilings and walls — the last surviving examples in Edinburgh. It also contains two wooden-shuttered booths.

## 9th

**1909:** Robert Garioch, sharp-eyed observer of the follies and foibles of his native city, was born in Edinburgh. "Embro to the Ploy" describes the city's literary pubs during the Festival.

> *The Café Royal and Abbotsford*
> *are filled wi orra folk*
> *whaes stock-in-trade's the scrievit word,*
> *or twice-scrievit joke.*
> *Brains, weak or strang, in heavy beer,*
> *or ordinary, soak.*
> *Quo yin: This yill is aafie dear,*
> *I hae nae clinks in poke,*
>     *nor fauldan money,*
> *in Embro to the ploy.*

# May

10th ———————————————————————————————

11th ———————————————————————————————

12th ———————————————————————————————

# May

## 10th

**1566:** Mary, Queen of Scots, granted a Royal Charter to the organisation now known as the Corporation of the Masters and Assistants of the Trinity House of Leith, which had been founded earlier to levy twelve pennies Scots on every ton of merchandise loaded or unloaded in the port of Leith. The purpose of this levy, "prime gilt" as it was called, was to provide relief for the poor, the aged and the infirm amongst the seafaring community. By the eighteenth century the Corporation had become concerned with the safe navigation of the sea approaches to the River Forth and in 1797 a charter was granted to them giving them the responsibility for the pilotage of the North Sea ports. The Corporation's present handsome hall was opened in 1817 in the Kirkgate in the port of Leith.

## 11th

**1935:** Over 10,000 people attended the opening ceremony of the new bandstand and open-air auditorium in Princes Street Gardens. Built as a memorial to the King's Silver Jubilee celebrations, the bandstand was the gift of the Distillers' Company whose chairman, W. H. Ross, gave his name to the new structure and who performed the opening ceremony. The open-air auditorium was designed to seat an audience of 2,000 and each summer there are concerts given by military and dance bands. The architects of the new building claimed that it had been constructed in such a way to throw out sound so that, were it not for the rumble of trams in Princes Street, the audience would be able to hear even the most *pianissimo* of movements.

## 12th

**1899:** In recognition of the part he had played in the Sudan War, the Town Council entertained to lunch the distinguished soldier Major-General Sir Hector Macdonald. One of the best-known military men of his day, Macdonald's career had begun as a private soldier in the Gordon Highlanders. There he had risen to the rank of sergeant and his bravery in the Afghan campaign earned him a commission in the same regiment. Following a successful rise through the commissioned ranks he became a general and aide de camp to the Queen — no mean achievement for an officer without social connections or private means. But the career of "Fighting Mac" — as he was popularly known — ended in tragedy in 1903. Accused of homosexuality in Ceylon he took his own life and lies buried in the Dean Cemetery in Edinburgh.

# May

13th _____

14th _____

15th _____

# May

## 13th

**1903:** Almost six years to the day after building had commenced, the new Fever Hospital was opened by King Edward VII. As long ago as the mid-nineteenth century public health officials, especially Dr Henry Littlejohn, had criticised the insanitary and overcrowded nature of much of Edinburgh's houses and had pressed the need for an isolation hospital to deal with the more chronic infectious diseases. After a good deal of lengthy discussion, Edinburgh Corporation bought a seventy-two-acre site on the former farm at Colinton Mains and plans were drawn up to construct a hospital for 750 patients. In its day it was the most modern hospital of its kind with its ample open spaces and warm red sandstone architecture. Today it is known as the City Hospital and it still deals with the care of infectious diseases.

## 14th

**1660:** The Restoration of King Charles II to the throne of Britain was proclaimed at the Mercat Cross amidst great scenes of jubilation. Edinburgh had enjoyed a much needed period of peace and calm during the reign of Cromwell but the opportunity to indulge in public revelry was too great a temptation to pass up. Sir George Mackenzie, the Lord Advocate, has left a telling description of the scenes he witnessed in the Royal Mile: "Wine was sent in abundance to the earth, that it might drink his majestie's health also, and the glasses capreoled in the air, for joy to hear his name. Some danced through the fire, knowing that the wine had so much modified them, that they need not fear burning; and others had bonfires kindled in their faces by the wine they had drunk."

## 15th

**1907:** At a cost of £40,000, the distinctive Princes Street store of R. W. Forsyth was opened on a site that had once been the town house of Hugo Arnot, one of Edinburgh's most distinguished eighteenth-century historians. The design of the building incorporated large open selling areas on different floors, a warehouse, and a distinctive feature was the good use made of the display windows at steet level. A good deal of carved stonework and bronze statues adorned the building and an interesting architectural innovation was that Forsyth's was the first building in Edinburgh to have been constructed on the American principle of steel upright and transverse beams embedded in concrete. Until its sad demise in 1981 Forsyth's was still one of the leading Princes Street stores.

# May

16th _____

17th _____

18th _____

# May

## 16th

**1975:** Under the terms of the Local Government (Scotland) Act of 1973, Edinburgh lost its identity as the "County of the City of Edinburgh" and in the local government reorganisation that followed it became a District of the newly formed Lothian Region. The District of the City of Edinburgh, as it had become, added to its domain the burgh of South Queensferry and the suburbs of Currie and Cramond. This was the latest in a long line of extensions to the city that had begun in 1767 with the Act extending the Ancient Royalty. Other additions to Edinburgh have been those of Portobello in 1896 and Leith in 1920, the year in which Edinburgh also extended itself to include the village suburbs of Corstorphine, Colinton, Swanston, Liberton, Juniper Green and Newhaven.

## 17th

**1718:** The tower of Old Greyfriars Church was accidentally blown up following a decision by the Town Council to store a supply of gunpowder in it. The cause of the explosion was never discovered but the damage was so great that the city authorities had no option but to build a new church at the east end of the old one rather than pay out a large sum simply to repair the tower. The old church had been built in 1612 on the grounds of the monastery of the same name and it was there that the National Covenant had been signed in 1638. A further calamity struck Old Greyfriars in January 1845 when a huge fire raged within the building leaving it nothing but a shell. The church was rebuilt at great expense and was adorned with several memorial windows including one to George Buchanan.

## 18th

**1843:** Following a lengthy dispute over the proper government of the Church of Scotland, there was a momentous interruption to the proceedings of the Church's General Assembly which is held annually in Edinburgh. After the Assembly had adjourned to St Andrew's Church in George Street, the Moderator, Dr Welsh, led out two hundred of his supporters amongst the clergy and they marched down Dundas Street to the Tanfield Hall in Canonmills where the Free Church of Scotland was set up with the reformer Thomas Chalmers as Moderator. The seceders separated themselves from the established Church of Scotland and the Disruption, as their dramatic walk-out came to be known, was to have an imposing effect on the young church which still meets in the city at the same time of year.

# May

19th _____

20th _____

21st_____

# May

## 19th

**1537:** Five months after his marriage to Madeleine, the daughter of the King of France, in the Cathedral Church of Notre Dame in Paris, King James V landed with his bride at the port of Leith. The historian John Leslie remarked on the new Queen's desire to please her adopted country and when she set foot ashore "she bowit and inclinit hir self to the earth and tuik the mullis thairof and kissit". Within forty days she was dead and making a barren mockery of Sir Richard Maitland's poetic words of welcome:

> *Excellent Princes! potent and preclair,*
> *Prudent, peerless in bontie and bewtie!*
> *Maist nobil Quein of Bluid under the air!*
> *With all my hairt and micht, I welcum the*
> *Hame to thy native pepill, and cuntrie.*

## 20th

**1780:** John Wesley, who, with his brother Charles, had founded a "methodist" society of pious young men, visited Edinburgh during one of his tireless tours around Britain. He admitted to his *Journal* that he "was not a preacher for the people of Edinburgh", but on the Saturday he was able to take "one more walk through Holyroodhouse, the mansion of ancient kings: but how melancholy an appearance does it make now! The stately rooms are dirty as stables: the colours of the tapestry are quite faded; several of the pictures are cut and defaced. The roof of the royal chapel is fallen in; and the bones of James the fifth, and the once beautiful Lord Darnley are scattered about like those of sheep or oxen. Such is human greatness! Is not a living dog better than a dead lion?"

## 21st

**1650:** Having returned to Scotland with a small Royalist army in support of Charles II, the Marquis of Montrose was defeated at Carbisdale and was taken to Edinburgh to face the death sentence passed in his absence in 1644. He was "to be carried to Edinburgh Cross, and hanged up, on a Gallows Thirty Feet high for the space of three hours, and then to be taken down, and his head to be cut off upon a Scaffold and hanged on Edinburgh Tolbooth, his legs and arms to be hanged up in other Towns of the Kingdom". Montrose faced his awful death with a dignity that survived even the taunts of his great enemy the Earl of Argyll as the procession passed his town residence at Moray House in the Canongate. Lady Argyll is supposed to have spat in Montrose's face when the tumbril stopped outside her window.

# May

22nd _____

23rd _____

24th _____

# May

## 22nd

**1859:** Arthur Conan Doyle, the creator of the great fictional detective Sherlock Holmes, was born in a house, now demolished, at 11 Picardy Place. His father was a clerk of works at Holyroodhouse and a devout Catholic who sent his son to school at Stonyhurst in England. From there Conan Doyle returned to Edinburgh to study medicine in the class of Dr Joseph Bell, a pioneer in forensic medicine who was to become one of the models for Sherlock Holmes. During his student days Conan Doyle lived in a small flat in Howe Street and on graduating he set up practice in the Portsmouth suburb of Southsea, but his memory of the insanitary horrors of the Old Town and his knowledge of forensic science stood him in good stead for his future career as a writer of detective fiction.

## 23rd

**1848:** During the demolition of Trinity College Church to make way for the railway station that was later to become Waverley Station, owned by the North British Railway Company, a coffin was found containing the remains of Mary of Gueldres, widow of James II and the founder of the church in 1462, a year before her own death. The church was the second collegiate foundation in the city and it provided a hospice for the poor as well as being a substantially endowed church school. The remains of Mary of Gueldres, who had married James II in 1449, were reinterred within the grounds of the Abbey of Holyrood. Mary's church had been dedicated to "the Holy Trinity, to the ever blessed and glorious Virgin Mary, to St Ninian the Confessor and to all the saints and elect people of God".

## 24th

**1661:** Almost eleven years to the day that he had watched his great rival the Marquis of Montrose go to a terrible death, the Earl of Argyll was himself executed at the Mercat Cross in Edinburgh. His support of Cromwell during the Commonwealth cost him his life although many of the people who had given evidence against him had been pro-government and anti-Royalist. As he awaited his death in the prison of the Castle, almost the last sounds he heard were the bells ringing and the guns blasting in honour of the official rehabilitation and reburial of the remains of Montrose. Before his execution he addressed the crowd. "I could die as a Roman but choose rather to die as a Christian." After his death his head was fixed on a pole above the Tolbooth where it was left to rot.

# May

25th _____

26th _____

27th _____

# May

## 25th

**1896:** The Lord Provost, Sir Andrew Macdonald, laid the foundation stone for the construction of the new North Bridge whose sweeping iron arches bind the old town to the new at the eastern end of Princes Street. The first bridge had been built by June 1769 across the valley of the Nor' Loch and it was seen by the early planners as an integral part of maintaining the unity of the growing city, but it was a poor design and it collapsed in August that same year killing five people. Financial wrangles prevented immediate repairs being made to the bridge and it was not until 1772 that it was opened again to traffic, and to pedestrians whose safety was assured by the introduction of a decent balustrade. The new metal bridge was opened in 1897 and a memorial tablet tells the story of its past.

## 26th

**1799:** James Burnett, Lord Monboddo, died at the age of eighty-five. Although stage coaches plied between Edinburgh and London, until the previous year this sturdy judge had preferred to ride on horseback to London when business summoned him to the south. But that was nothing out of the ordinary to this eccentric man of law: throughout his life, on rainy days, he would walk bare-headed while his wig rode dry inside an accompanying sedan chair. Like many of his fellow lords of the Court of Session, Monboddo was a philosopher and an historian. He also believed that men were originally monkeys and he held to a belief that women had vestigial tails, and Samuel Johnson remarked of him that "Monboddo is as jealous of his tale as a squirrel". Rumour had it that he kept a flute-playing orang-utan.

## 27th

**1826:** A meeting of twenty-four artists under the chairmanship of George Watson agreed to found a Royal Scottish Academy of Painting, Sculpture and Architecture. The Academy amalgamated with the Royal Institution and used the latter's imposing building at the foot of the Mound as their first headquarters. That building had been founded in 1823 and it was improved and enlarged by William Playfair who also designed the neighbouring National Galleries of Scotland. With its dramatic Doric fluted columns projecting into Princes Street, the building drew a good deal of adverse comment, especially in later years when a massive statue of Queen Victoria was added to crown its facade. The first annual exhibition of the Royal Scottish Academy was held in February 1827.

# May

28th _____

29th _____

30th _____

# May

## 28th

**1329:** Edinburgh's Royal Charter was presented to the city by
King Robert the Bruce, the victor of the Battle of Bannockburn,
just ten days before his death on 7th June at Cardross in Fife.
Written in Latin, the parchment, which is still extant, set out the
city's rights and granted to the people of Edinburgh control of
the port of Leith and also of the burgh's mills which stood
by the Water of Leith in what is now the Dean Village. To
mark the six hundredth anniversary of the granting of the
charter two massive statues representing the Scottish patriots,
King Robert the Bruce, by Thomas J. Clapperton, and Sir William
Wallace, by Alexander Carrick, were unveiled by the Duke
of York, later King George VI, to stand guard at the gates of
the Castle.

## 29th

**1839:** "From an early age I have felt a strong interest in Edinburgh,
though attached to Edinburgh by no other ties than those which
are common to me with multitudes; that tie which attaches every
man of Scottish blood to the ancient and renowned capital of
our race; that tie which attaches every student of history to the spot
ennobled by so many great and memorable events; that tie
which attaches every traveller of taste to the most beautiful of
British cities; and that tie which attaches every lover of literature
to a place which, since it has ceased to be the seat of empire, has
derived from poetry, philosophy, and eloquence a far higher
distinction than empire can bestow." That speech was made by
Lord Macaulay who acted as Member of Parliament for the city,
between 1839-47 and 1852-56.

## 30th

**1977:** The new runway and terminal buildings were opened at
Turnhouse, the airport that serves Edinburgh. With its longer and
more durable runway, Turnhouse was finally able to cater for
the new generation of jet aircraft that most airlines had begun to
operate since the late nineteen-sixties. For many years aircraft
using the old runway which runs east-west had been bedevilled by
crosswinds and by the updraughts caused by the Pentland Hills,
and although the airport became safer it became more impersonal,
with many travellers regretting the loss of the smaller, more
intimate terminal building. The busiest route from Edinburgh
is the trunk route to London, but there is also a reasonable selection
of flights to other English and Scottish destinations and to cities
in Ireland and Europe.

# May

**1878:** Eugene Chantrelle was the first murderer to be hanged in Edinburgh away from the public gaze after Parliament had decided that public executions belonged properly to a more barbarous age. His crime was the murder of his wife Lizzie, by the slow application of gas, in their house in George Street, and Chantrelle almost succeeded in covering up the true facts of her death. Despite some vigorous pleading by Chantrelle, he was sentenced to death and on the eve of his execution he showed something of his style by asking the governor of Calton Jail to provide him with three bottles of champagne and a whore. Although there would be nothing for them to see, a large crowd gathered on Calton Hill on a bright sunlit summer morning hoping to catch a glimpse of the sombre proceedings within the jail.

# June

At the east end of Princes Street stands Calton Hill. It has become an open-air museum of monuments with Nelson's inverted telescope, monuments to Robert Burns and Dugald Stewart, and the hill is dominated by the pillars of Scotland's failed parthenon, an uncompleted memorial to the dead of the Napoleonic wars.

# June

1st _____

2nd _____

3rd _____

# June

## 1st

**1903:** The world famous floral clock at the corner of Princes Street Gardens, near the Mound, at the base of Allan Ramsay's statue, continued to give pleasure in the days after its unveiling. In those early days it only had an hour hand as the original clock was a reject from Elie Parish Church in Fife, but another hand was added the following year and the cuckoo mechanism was introduced in 1905. The clock did good service until its retirement in 1936 when it was replaced by a more modern device. Each year the clock is covered with up to 25,000 flowers and shrubs and the design is usually of a topical nature reflecting an important national or international event. It remains one of the city's most popular tourist attractions and the annual floral theme is kept a secret until the clock is decked out in spring.

## 2nd

**1575:** "By reason of his great infirmitie and seiknes" the aged Lord Home was carried from his imprisonment in the Castle to die in a lodging house at the head of Blackfriars Wynd that was later to become the town house of the Clerks of Penicuik. Two years earlier, Home, a loyal supporter of Mary Queen of Scots, had surrendered the Castle to Sir William Drury. Home's companions, including the noble commander of the garrison, Sir William Kirkcaldy of Grange, were executed but he was condemned to eke out his years in close confinement in the Castle. Two Edinburgh goldsmiths who had minted coins for the defenders, James Mossman and James Cokir, were also executed at the Mercat Cross with the other leaders. A memorial tablet in the Castle roadway commemorates Grange and his stalwart defence.

## 3rd

**1674:** The Town Council heard a petition, which proved unsuccessful, to remove the City Guard House to a position in the High Street opposite Stevenlaw's Close near the Tron Kirk. It was a long black-slated building of four apartments which had been built during the Cromwellian occupation of the city and it tended to be a noisy raucous place when drunks and common thieves were rounded up by the City Guard late at night. At the west end of the building stood a wooden hobby horse to which drunkards were tied with heavy drinking cups on their heads. The building was eventually demolished in 1784. Behind it stood for many years the mansion of a former provost of the city, Sir Simon Preston of Craigmillar. It had been built as early as 1461 and was known as the Black Turnpike.

# June

4th _____

5th _____

6th _____

# June

## 4th

**1658:** Beer has been brewed in Edinburgh since the twelfth century when the monks of the Canongate discovered that the water there was admirably suited to the brewing of the heavy beer that is the staple ale in Scotland. It was a popular drink, too, and when in 1658 the Town Council found itself unable to maintain its schools and hospitals, it raised a tax of "four pennyis scotts upon every pyntt of aill and beere brewed, sold or spent within this Cittie". The councillors reasoned that a general tax would discourage investment and business within the city, whereas a tax on beer would be — like the commodity — easily swallowed by the city's topors. Beer is still brewed in the Canongate by Scottish and Newcastle Brewers who produce the world famous Younger's and McEwan's beers.

## 5th

**1723:** Although his place of birth was the town of Kirkcaldy in Fife, the name of the political economist Adam Smith is inextricably bound up with the Enlightenment period in Edinburgh. He arrived in the city in 1748 and became acquainted immediately with some of the leading intellectuals — or *literati* as they styled themselves — such as the law lord, Lord Kames, and the philosopher David Hume. At the University he lectured on Rhetoric and Belles Lettres but in 1751 he moved to Glasgow to become Professor of Logic and Moral Philosophy. His connections with Edinburgh, though, were maintained through his memberships of the Poker Club and the Select Society which were then two of the city's leading debating clubs. His great work, *The Wealth of Nations*, was published in 1776 and on his retiral he lived in Edinburgh until his death in 1790.

## 6th

**1938:** "If the authorities in Edinburgh forgot what R. L. Stevenson wrote about the city with its high altar of winds when they carried out their decorative schemes in Princes Street for the display of burgh banners they have had a boisterous reminder. The wind blew steadily from the south all day, reaching gale force at times. By the time it had spent its unseasonable fury the burgh banners emerged from this war of the elements about as tattered as some of the banners which have been carried into battle and now adorn the walls of St Giles Cathedral." *The Scotsman* was reporting, somewhat caustically, on the damage done to the 84 Scots burgh banners which had been hung in Princes Street as decorations to honour the annual General Assembly of the Church of Scotland.

# June

7th _____

8th _____

9th _____

# June

## 7th

**1934:** As the discussions about the removal of the iron railings to Princes Street Gardens continued to rage in Edinburgh, on the day of decision, few bothered to remember the history of the gardens themselves which today extend to about nine acres in the city centre. They form part of what was once the Nor' Loch and include the property known as Bearford's Parks which were purchased by the Town Council in 1717. The loch was drained in 1763 when the sluice gates were opened for the last time and the site of the loch quickly dried out. In 1844 the site was let to a nurseryman but his reign was short lived as that same year work began on the railway cutting that linked the Waverley and Haymarket stations. Since 1876 the gardens have been in the care of the Town Council.

## 8th

**1681:** A minute of the Town Council of Edinburgh regarding the election of captains for the Trained Bands showed that although the burgh of the Canongate was under the jurisdiction of a separate council, Edinburgh continued to exert a considerable influence over the affairs of its close neighbour. Under the original charter of the Canongate, the canons of Holyrood were the first superiors but their position was removed from them after the Reformation in 1587 and the superiority passed into the hands of private families. In 1636 the Town Council of Edinburgh gained possession and one of the three Baron Bailies of the burgh of the Canongate was appointed by Edinburgh. In 1856 the councils of the two burghs merged into one but the Canongate, with its more spacious lands, still retains much of its original identity.

## 9th

**1890:** The Edinburgh Central Public Library on George IV Bridge was opened by Lord Rosebery, almost exactly three years to the month after its foundations had been laid. Built to a design by Sir George Washington Browne, the library owed its existence to a gift from Andrew Carnegie, the Dunfermline-born millionaire who had used his fortune to endow so many educational institutions in Scotland. The library is an imposing building constructed on the site of the seventeenth-century town house of Sir Thomas Hope, Lord Advocate to Charles I. Two lintels from that original building have been preserved above the internal doorways. The adjoining Fine Art library is housed in the former Highland Institute, and it is worth noting the Edinburgh Room, a mine of information about the city's heritage.

# June

10th _____

11th _____

12th _____

# June

10th _____

**1861:** The first firing of the time gun from the Half Moon Battery in the Castle at one o'clock has its origins in the decision of the Leith Dock Commission to press for the location of a time ball on the Nelson Monument on Calton Hill in 1854. Plans to synchronise the dropping of the ball at one o'clock with an audible signal were finalised in January 1861. The Chamber of Commerce arranged for a 4,000-feet telegraph wire to be strung across Edinburgh from the Calton Hill to the Castle and since the summer of 1861 the boom of the one o'clock gun has announced the time of day to complacent citizens and to astonished visitors. The gun is now fired electrically from the Royal Observatory on Blackford Hill and its longest silence was during the period of the Second World War.

11th _____

**1788:** The South Bridge over the Cowgate, which runs from the High Street to Nicolson Street, was opened to traffic. Under its south pier in the Cowgate disappeared the tavern known as Lucky Middlemass, which was one of the favourite haunts of the poet Robert Fergusson. A year later work was begun on the new University building designed by Robert Adam and later modified by William Playfair. It opened in 1815 and is now known as Old College. Shops began to spring up along both sides of the bridge and it became something of a publishers' and booksellers' quarter in the late eighteenth and early nineteenth centuries, a reputation it keeps to this day with the shop of James Thin, one of Britain's leading firms of booksellers, which has been there since 1848.

12th _____

**1678:** "The councill being informed that James Sympsone skipper and seaverall merchants that are to take part with him are resolved to build at Leith ane ship of the burding of thrie hundred tuns and to munt hir with fourtie guns or thereby which will not onlie tend to the benefit and advantage of the carpenters and other workmen in South and North Leith But will also much ten to the credit of the Kingdome in respect that the lyke ship as to hir burding and number of gunes hes not been built in Scotland these many years bygone." Leith has remained a centre for shipbuilding and ship repairs but the most magnificent ship to have been built in Edinburgh was the *Great Michael*. Commissioned by King James IV it was built in Newhaven and half of Fife's woods were supposed to have been used in its construction.

# June

13th _____

14th _____

15th _____

# June

## 13th

**1831:** In a house at 14 India Street, the future scientist James Clerk Maxwell was born into a family that had estates in Glenlair, Galloway. His childhood was divided between the two places, with summers spent on the estate, and he was educated at the Edinburgh Academy. Regarded as the father of modern science, Maxwell held professorships at Aberdeen and London before he became the first holder of the Cavendish Chair of Experimental Physics at Cambridge. His pioneering work on gases, optics and the nature of colour laid the foundation for future discoveries in electricity and in magnetism and paved the way for the development of the radio and of colour photography. His training as a scientist owed much to the Edinburgh philosophical tradition. He died early, at the age of forty-eight.

## 14th

**1905:** The first company to introduce motor bus services in the Edinburgh area, the Scottish Motor Traction Company (S.M.T.), was formed with an authorised capital of £50,000. For some years it had become obvious that the combination of trams and horse buses could not cope with the needs of Edinburgh's travelling public and yet the combustion engine was not at the stage of development where it could be used as a reliable means of traction. S.M.T. experimented with several different types of vehicle before inaugurating their services and it was not until 1st January 1906 that the first route — between the Mound and Corstorphine — was inaugurated, using Maudslay double-deckers. By the following year S.M.T. was able to introduce new services to Cramond and farther afield to Queensferry and Dalkeith.

## 15th

**1633:** King Charles I entered the city of Edinburgh on a visit that was to be the last *official* visit by a British monarch until George IV's visit of 1822. He was met at the West Port by the spirit of Edina, and Fergus, the legendary King of Scotland, received him at the Tolbooth with an address full of suitable words of advice. The Town Council accompanied Charles to Holyroodhouse and he was crowned King of Scotland in the neighbouring abbey two days later. Although the purpose of his visit was a pacific one and Edinburgh responded with its customary pageantry and hospitality, the ulterior motive behind Charles's triumphant entry was the subjugation of the Church of Scotland to the episcopalian pattern of church government and order of service.

# June

16th _____

17th _____

18th _____

# June

## 16th

**1821:** At the burial of John Ballantyne in the Canongate churchyard Sir Walter Scott turned to his son-in-law, John Gibson Lockhart, and whispered "I feel as if there would be less sunshine for me from this day henceforth." Ballantyne had been a partner in the publishing and printing business which had been established by his brother James and Scott, but it had not worked out as a viable business proposition. The latter years of his life had been spent as an auctioneer and he also wrote a sentimental novel, *The Widow's Lodging*. The Ballantynes came from Kelso and had been school friends of Scott's. It was that close relationship that led to the establishment of James's printing business and later the partnership with Scott's publisher, Archibald Constable.

## 17th

**1790:** One of the most striking beauties in Edinburgh during its Golden Age was Elizabeth Burnett, the daughter of the eccentric judge Lord Monboddo. But the cold damp winters in Edinburgh were unkind to her fragile health and her death at Braid Farm to the south of the city touched Robert Burns to write a graceful elegy from distant Dumfries:

> *We saw thee shine in youth and beauty's pride,*
> *And Virtue's light, that beams beyond the spheres;*
> *But like the sun eclipsed at morning-tide,*
> *Thou left'st us darkling in a world of tears.*

Burns met Elizabeth in Edinburgh in 1787, and as Alison Cockburn, who wrote "The Flowers of the Forest", noted: "His favourite for looks and manners is Bess Burnett—no bad judge indeed."

## 18th

**1846:** Following the establishment of the North British Railway, the company opened its principal station in Edinburgh and named it Waverley after the novels of Sir Walter Scott. The station lay at the east end of the valley that once housed the Nor' Loch and two months later it was linked to Haymarket through Princes Street Gardens and the construction of two tunnels. The station was extended between 1869 and 1873 and it was reconstructed completely at the end of the nineteenth century, heralding in the 1900s with its fine glass roofs and elegant booking hall. From Waverley the great Anglo-Scottish expresses, such as The Flying Scotsman and The Talisman, linked — and continue to do so even in these days of the high-speed train — Edinburgh with London.

# June

19th _____

20th _____

21st_____

# June

## 19th

**1566:** In a small wood-panelled room in the south-east corner of the Palace Lodgings in Edinburgh Castle, Mary Queen of Scots gave birth to an infant son, the future James VI of Scotland and I of Great Britain. His father was Mary's second husband, the weak-willed Lord Darnley, who was to be murdered within nine months at the House of Kirk of Field. Mary's part in that escapade together with her hasty marriage to the powerful fourth Earl of Bothwell, was to alienate her from her supporters. On her abdication in 1567, James was proclaimed King and during the period of his minority he was kept in Stirling. There his tutors were George Buchanan and Peter Young who gave him a grounding in poetry and the classics. James succeeded to the throne of Scotland at the age of thirteen.

## 20th

**1701:** The Advocates' Library, which had been founded in 1682 by Sir George Mackenzie of Rosehaugh, had been destroyed by fire in 1700 and the Faculty of Advocates applied, successfully as it turned out, to the Town Council for additional space in Parliament House. "Upon reprt of Baillie Clark that the Magistrats had frequentlie met with the facultie of advocats who are craveing that a pairt of the laigh parliament house might be allowed to them (during the Councils pleasure) for a Librarie to accommodate the books of the facultie The Councill are most willing to mentaine and perpetuat the good understanding and friendship now betuixt the good toun and said facultie. . . ." The Advocates' Library became the National Library of Scotland in 1925 and its present home is on George IV Bridge.

## 21st

**1689:** The Town Council agreed that it should borrow "nyne Thousand merks Scottis money toward the payment of that soume aggreed to be payed to Mr James Smith for building of the Canongate Kirk". The Canongate kirk had been built in the previous year to house the congregation that had been ousted from Holyroodhouse, and it is one of the city's finest places of worship. With a Dutch influence in its design it is cruciform in shape and fronted by an elegant facade which boasts the Royal coat of arms above the main entrance. It was here that Bonnie Prince Charlie held prisoner the English officers captured after the Battle of Prestonpans in 1745 but today the church is perhaps best known for its graveyard where sleep the remains of the poet Robert Fergusson and the creator of *The Wealth of Nations*, Adam Smith.

# June

22nd _____

23rd _____

24th _____

# June

## 22nd

**1649:** George Winram, an advocate and a leading spokesman for the General Assembly of the Church of Scotland, was appointed Lord Liberton for his services in negotiating the return of Charles II to Scotland. He took part in the Battle of Dunbar in 1650 but died of his wounds a few days later. The Winrams were the owners of Inch House in Craigmillar which was known by that name as it was one of the only houses in Edinburgh to be surrounded by a watered moat. The area of the Inch belonged originally to the monks of the Abbey of Holyrood. The earliest date on the house is 1617 and the initials show that it belonged to the Winram family which came originally from Clydesdale. The house stands today in the public park in the modern suburb of Liberton.

## 23rd

**1829:** At a cost of £34,000 the new buildings of the Royal High School were opened in Regent Road below Calton Hill. They had been designed by a former pupil, Thomas Hamilton, and the classical design, with its central portico and great hall, was based on the Temple of Theseus in Athens. A great procession of the boys and masters was joined by the Town Council with the Lord Provost and representatives of the University and they led the way from the old High School buildings in the yards near the Cowgate preceded by a military band. The school remained in Hamilton's building until 1968 when it was removed to a modern construction in the suburb of Barnton. Subsequently, Hamilton's building was refurbished during the nineteen-seventies to house the ill-fated, still-born Scottish Assembly.

## 24th

**1767:** For the benefit of trade and commerce and for the common good of the citizens, an Act was passed on the instigation of the Town Council to extend the ancient royalty or boundaries of the city. It was agreed to purchase the following lands: 36 acres of the barony of Broughton, 32 acres of the lands of Bearford's Parks, 6 acres of the lands of Moultreeshill, the lands of Forglen's and Allan's Parks and the lands of Calton Hill, Greenside and Picardy. The chief portion included the original New Town from Princes Street to Fettes Row and from Calton Hill to Charlotte Square. The other portions are situated in the present areas of Haymarket, the West End, Warriston, Broughton Road, Abbeyhill and St Leonards. Edinburgh underwent several further extensions in the eighteenth century.

# June

25th _____

26th _____

27th _____

# June

## 25th

**1841:** At a dinner attended by more than three hundred excited guests, the Magistrates and Town Council of the City of Edinburgh presented the novelist Charles Dickens with the freedom of the city. Dickens was already familiar with the city having visited it in 1834 to cover the celebrations for the passing of the Reform Bill and he was to return frequently to give readings from his novels in the Music Hall. After one such reading in 1858 he reminded his audience that it was Edinburgh, of all the cities in Britain, that had first offered him the honour of making him a freeman. "You will readily believe that I have carried into the various countries I have since traversed and through all my subsequent career, the proud and affectionate remembrance of that eventful epoch in my life."

## 26th

**1634:** One of the most entertaining descriptions of early Edinburgh was written by Sir William Brereton who passed through the city on his way to Glasgow: "I took a view of the castle here, which is seated very high and sufficiently commanding, and being able to batter the town; this is also seated upon the top of a most hard rock, and the passage whereunto was (as they here report) made through that hard and impregnable rock, which cannot be touched or hewed, and it is indeed a stately passage, wherein was used more industry, pains, art and endeavour, than in any place I have found amongst the Scotts. It is but a very little castle, of no great receipt, but mighty strength; it is called castrum puellarum, because the kings of the Picts kept their virgins therein. . . ."

## 27th

**1659:** Twenty-five years after the death of "Jinglin' Geordie", George Heriot, jeweller to King James VI, a school built in his name and from his mighty fortunes was opened in Lauriston. It dominates the southern skyline when viewed from the Castle esplanade and its fine Renaissance lines include a central quadrangle, romantically turreted corner towers and a plethora of smaller octagonal towers. George Heriot's School is one of the largest private schools in the city and over the years it has maintained high academic standards with a more recent standing in sport, especially rugby football. The remaining buildings in the school yard date from more recent times. In 1650 the main building was used by Cromwell's troops as a hospital and it remained in that capacity until 1658.

# June

28th _____

29th _____

30th _____

# June

## 28th

**1838:** On Queen Victoria's Coronation Day, Granton Harbour, which had been developed through the expense of the fifth Duke of Buccleuch, was declared open. The harbour boasted a pier to be used "by vessels of the largest class", steam cranes, a slipway and a breakwater 3,000 feet in length. The harbour was used for trading and a customs house and hotel were added later; it also came to be used by a small fleet of fishing trawlers. Although the harbour is today used mainly as a place of recreation, being a yachting marina, it did once boast the world's first passenger train ferries. In February 1850 the Edinburgh and Northern Railway opened through services from Edinburgh to Fife by loading carriages onto the ferry *Leviathan* and transporting them to Burntisland. The operation ceased in 1890.

## 29th

**1559:** The man who stood behind the Reformation Movement in Scotland, John Knox, preached for the first time in the Church of St Giles. Knox was born in the neighbouring East Lothian town of Haddington and had worked in his home area as a priest until 1545 when he met the visionary reformer George Wishart. Following the debacle of the murder of Cardinal Beaton in St Andrews, Knox had been a galley slave of the French and had lived for a time in Geneva before returning to Edinburgh where he became eventually a minister of the newly formed Protestant church. The strength of his personality and his fiercely held beliefs helped to convert many Scots men and women to his cause and during the reign of Mary, Queen of Scots, he was an implacable enemy of the court.

## 30th

**1823:** The foundation stone of the Edinburgh Academy was laid by the president of the directors, Robert Dundas of Arniston, on a piece of land in Henderson Row that had been feued from the governors of George Heriot's Hospital. Amongst the directors were Lord Cockburn and Sir Walter Scott, and the intention of the founders was that the Academy should provide an education solidly rooted in the classics. It would charge higher fees than the High School and it was also to be modelled on the English public school system. Designed by William Burn, the Edinburgh Academy is a somewhat plain building, with a low pillared portico, but it boasts a splendid oval hall and a spacious school-yard. The school opened in October 1824, and remains one of the country's leading schools.

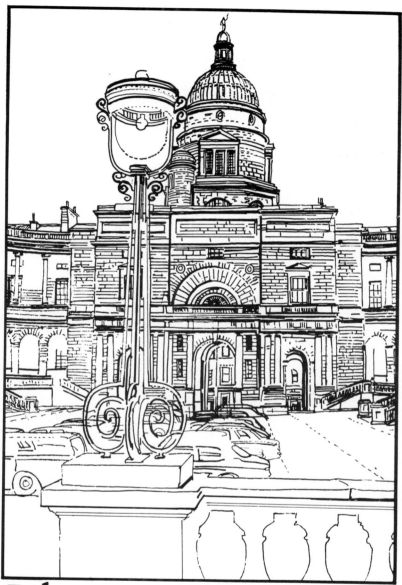

# July

Edinburgh's university was founded in 1582 by Royal Charter and today is one of the largest in Britain with a particular leaning to medical research. The main building is William Playfair's Old College on South Bridge.

# July

1st _____

2nd _____

3rd _____

# July

## 1st

**1531:** The Town Council kept a close watch on the quality of goods and produce offered for sale in the burgh. Transgressions were punished severely. "The provest, baillies and counsale, sittand in jugement, decernys and ordanis David Gillaspye baxter, for braking of the statutis of the toun oft and sindrie tymes, baikand his breid unsufficient stuf bayth of wecht and fynes, and wald nocht mend the samyn bot persaverit dailie thairintill, for the quhilk cause he sal pay to the commoun gude the sowme of ten pundis; and gyf he happinis fale in tyme cuming anent the baiking of his breid, contrair the statutis of the toun, thay ordane he be spanyt the occupatioun of the baxter craft for all the dayis of his lyfe."

## 2nd

**1636:** The Greenhill Estate, which adjoined Bruntsfield Links and which is still remembered in the names of the streets in the area, was bought from its original owners the Aikenheads by John Livingston, a burgess and apothecary. His ownership did not last long as he was killed in the plague of 1645 and was buried in the grounds of his estate — the headstone erected by his wife still stands in Chamberlain Road. The mansion house of Greenhill was built in 1666 and before its demolition in 1884 it was a tiresome reminder of the window tax of 1696 as several of its thirty-two windows had to be blocked up as the tax became more punitive. The house is celebrated by a stone plaque carved by Washington Browne, an architect particularly associated with the area. It stands at the corner of Bruntsfield Gardens.

## 3rd

**1843:** Sir David Brewster, Principal of the University of St Andrews, wrote to the photographic pioneer Fox Talbot about the speculative partnership that had sprung up in Edinburgh between D. O. Hill and Robert Adamson for the manufacture of calotypes. From their studio at Rock House on Calton Hill the Hill-Adamson partnership produced an impressive number of early calotypes, glorious "sun pictures" as they called them, the forerunners of the modern photograph. Through their work, which began with making likenesses of sitters for Hill's painting of the Disruption, we have been left with a vivid record of the times they lived in and of the people they knew, from intellectual lions to the fisherfolk of Granton and Newhaven. Adamson's early death in 1848 brought the flourishing partnership to an end.

# July

4th _____

5th _____

6th _____

# July

## 4th

**1385:** "John, eldest son of the King, Earl of Carrick, and Steward of Scotland, To all who shall hear or see this charter, eternal salvation in the Lord. Know ye that we, by advice of our Council, have given, granted, and by this charter, have confirmed to our beloved and faithfull all and each the Burgesses of the Community of the Burgh of Edinburgh, having their dwellings, or wishing to construct their houses in the Castle of Edinburgh in future, that they, their heirs and servants, with their goods, victuals, and other necessaries whatsoever, entering, remaining, or going out of the said castle, shall have free ingress and egress, so that no fees whatever shall be paid to the constable or porter of the Castle provided that the said Burgesses be considered of good fame and honest conversation."

## 5th

**1828:** Dr Andrew Duncan, the founder of the city's first humanitarian lunatic asylum, died in Edinburgh and after a public funeral was buried in the little Buccleuch cemetery which nestles below the Appleton and Hume Towers in George Square. The asylum, now part of the Royal Edinburgh Hospital, was built on a site between Morningside Park and Maxwell Street and was known originally as the East House. As an apprentice, Duncan had been much affected by the sufferings of patients in the Edinburgh Bedlam which had stood behind the old city wall near the present-day Forrest Road and it was the death there in 1774 of the poet Robert Fergusson that resolved the young doctor to improve conditions for the mentally ill. Funds were slow in coming and it was not until 1807 that a Royal Charter was granted for the foundation of the hospital.

## 6th

**1746:** Tweeddale House in Tweeddale Court off the High Street, once the Edinburgh home of a noted Borders family, became the first headquarters of the British Linen Company which was founded by Royal Charter of King George II. Its intention was to promote the linen industry in Scotland and the company began its operations by importing flax. It was also heavily involved in the manufacture of linen and yarns. Gradually it began to withdraw from manufacturing and by 1763 it had taken over the responsibilities of a bank to the linen industry. The British Linen Bank, as it became, was one of the great Scottish clearing banks, issuing its own notes and opening over eighty branches throughout Scotland. Its name continues as the merchant banking house of Barclay's Bank.

# July

7th _____

8th _____

9th _____

# July

## 7th

**1675:** Andrew Balfour and Robert Sibbald, two of Edinburgh's earliest medical pioneers, successfully petitioned the Town Council to gain the lease of a piece of land adjoining Trinity Hospital at the east end of the Nor' Loch. The ground became the Physic Garden — in reality, the city's first botanic garden — and within its narrow confines Sibbald arranged for some 2,000 species of plants to be grown, many of which were planted for their medicinal properties. Together with James Sutherland, the first keeper, the two men were responsible for Edinburgh's early lead in botanical studies. In the mid-eighteenth century the garden moved to the west side of Leith Walk where now stands Haddington Place and in 1820 it moved to its present site at Inverleith. The first garden lies below Waverley Station.

## 8th

**1823:** At his house in Stockbridge, little more than a stone's throw from where he had been born, one of Scotland's greatest painters, Sir Henry Raeburn, died at the age of sixty-eight. Best known for his wonderfully luminous portraits of the leading men and women of his day, Raeburn captured much of the spirit of enquiry of the period of the Enlightenment, and was suitably rewarded with a knighthood in 1822 and by his appointment as King's Limner in Scotland. His studio was situated in 32 York Place and it was said of him that scarcely a patrician family in Scotland had not had at least one of its members sit for him there. Raeburn also had an interest in landscape gardening and was a keen marine architect, one of his sports being to sail large model boats in Warriston Pond.

## 9th

**1657:** A minute of the parish records of South Leith Church made first official mention of the need to provide a special pew for the magistrates of Leith: "it was ordered to build ane new seat to the Bailivies in the bodie of the Kirke before ther old seat". The custom must have passed into abeyance because when Leith was reconstituted as a burgh in 1833 by the Municipal Reform Act, one of the first acts of the new Town Council was to apply to the South Leith Church for permission to occupy the front seat of the maltsman's loft in what is now the organ gallery and it took an Act of Parliament of 1838 to restore to the Council the traditional pew "in the bodie of the Kirke". Although Leith lost its burgh status in 1920 the pew is still known as the "Magistrates' Pew".

# July

10th _____

11th _____

12th _____

# July

## 10th

**1696:** Unaware of the disaster that had befallen the Scottish colony in the narrow isthmus of Darien in Central America, the Town Council agreed "to subscrybe the books of the African and Indian Company for the sume of £3000 starling, and have appoynted his Lordship to signe the books of the said company for the forsaid sume . . .". The Darien Scheme, as it came to be known, had its origins in the desire of the Edinburgh merchants to break the monopoly of the East India Company and Darien was chosen as a trading colony because of its propinquity to the Pacific and Atlantic oceans. However, English indifference and Spanish hostility, together with the Scots' own lack of experience, led to financial disaster and to the forfeiture of the colony with a severe loss of life and property.

## 11th

**1788:** "Went to Mr Barclay's at 10 — Came out at $^1\!/_2$ past 12 and called on Hugh Watson — He was at the Play on Wednesday Evening — Came home at 2 o'clock — I hear that Brodie is arrived and that he is lodged in the Castle. A thick mist. Went to Mr B. at 5 o'clock. Came out at $^1\!/_2$ past 7. Called on Hugh Watson. Came home at 8. N.B. Mr John Watt married in his House to Miss Betsy Adams tonight. This day I wrote out a Receit to be given to James Milligan on delivering me my Prints etc." Although Edinburgh has spawned many diarists whose records offer a personal and intimate picture of the city in a bygone age, the reminiscences of George Sandy have a particular charm because he was a sixteen-year-old legal apprentice when he wrote his diary and his observations are a mixture of naivity and acute sensibility.

## 12th

**1828:** *The Scotsman* reported that the Rev. John Somerville, minister of Currie Church, had presented the King with a patent safety gun of his own invention "which was most graciously received and highly approved of by his Majesty". The church at Currie, a village lying to the south-west of Edinburgh but now part of the conurbation, was built in 1785 at a cost of £433 and the structure contains several earlier reliques such as the Calvary Stones which were unearthed at an ancient grave nearby, and the Templar Stone in one of the window sills which dates from the thirteenth century. A high steeple was added twenty-five years after the church opened and the clock and weather vane were gifted to the church in 1818 by the same Rev. Somerville of the Royal ordinance fame.

# July

13th _____

14th _____

15th _____

*John Knox's house and fountain well*

# July

## 13th

**1757:** Three years after it had been finally agreed that members of the Town Council should wear scarlet gowns, a minute records the Council's decision to honour an account for the supply of ermine skins furnished for the Lord Provost's gown. Form earliest times it had been the practice of the Town Council to wear robes that reflected the dignity of their positions and that marked out their rank. The practice was solemnised by Royal interest in the uniform of public officials and by the seventeenth century it was generally recognised that the Town Council would wear red gowns and the magistrates black although there was a time when all black was the order of the day. Councillors not wearing ceremonial garb were likely to face heavy fines.

## 14th

**1927:** The Scottish National War Memorial, which had caused such controversy in Edinburgh because it was sited within the ancient walls of the Castle and therefore altered the skyline, was opened at a dedicatory service by the Prince of Wales. The memorial is to the design of the distinguished Scottish architect Sir Robert Lorimer who died shortly after his last work was opened to the public. It contains an inner shrine which houses the tomb of the Unknown Soldier and the whole building is a monument in stone, bronze and illuminated glass dedicated to the memory of the men and women of Scotland who gave their lives in the First World War. "And there, hemmed in by so many insignias of sorrow," wrote Sir Ian Hamilton, "there lies the book (of honour) — and in that book, one hundred thousand names — Scotland for ever!"

## 15th

**1805:** The passing of the new Police Act in April 1805 effectively ended the existence of the City Guard which had come into being in 1696 as the leading body of law and order in the city. With their quaint cocked hats and Lochaber axes the Guard had presented a comic picture to the world and over the years they had gained a spectacular reputation for inefficiency and drunkenness. On the day that the Act came into force two companies of the City Guard were disbanded although one company of three officers, two drummers and thirty men remained in being until 1817 when the modern police force took over from their colourful predecessors the responsibility for the maintenance of law and order. The new Act also required all streets in the city to be named and all houses to be numbered.

# July

16th ————————————————————————————

17th ————————————————————————————

18th ————————————————————————————

# July

## 16th

**1890:** The foundation stone for Craighouse Asylum was laid by the tenth Earl of Stair and the building was opened four years later at a cost of £150,000. There had been considerable disquiet over the selling of the land for the new asylum and it ended the association with the area of the well-known historian Dr John Hill Burton, H.M. Historiographer for Scotland. From its foundation, and indeed until fairly recent times, the hospital was for the use of private patients and the building still retains much of its original sumptuous design, especially the Grand Hall which could almost be the entrance to a country house and not that of a hospital for the mentally ill. From the top of the tower, itself an imposing landmark, there are some of the best southern views of Edinburgh.

## 17th

**1695:** Following the establishment of the Bank of England in the previous year and the consequent agitation of Scottish businessmen for a bank of their own use, the Bank of Scotland came into being by Act of Parliament. Its first headquarters was in Mylne Square and its first governor was John Holland, an Englishman who was deemed to be a naturalised Scot! (By a quirk of fate, the Bank of England was founded by a Scot, William Paterson.) The fledgling bank issued its own notes, a practice it continues to this day. By the seventeen-thirties the Bank of Scotland had opened branches in Aberdeen, Dundee and Glasgow but the turning point came with the Industrial Revolution with the release of cash credits. The bank's present headquarters is the Roman-Corinthian building on the Mound.

## 18th

**1924:** The day after his graduation from the University of Edinburgh, the Olympic Games 400 metres champion Eric Liddell was given a public dinner in his honour. Although it was well meant and eulogy-laden, nothing could have matched the enthusiasm of his fellow students who had pulled Liddell in an open carriage through streets thronged with cheering crowds. Liddell was one of Scotland's most popular athletes, a sprinter of speed and power — though of ungainly style — who had gained international fame for his running in the 1924 Paris Olympic Games. Selected originally for the 100 metres, he refused the chance of winning a gold medal because the heats were to be run on a Sunday and ran instead in the 400 metres, winning it by five yards in a world record time of 47.6 seconds.

# July

19th _____

20th _____

21st_____

# July

## 19th

**1889:** After a good deal of controversy and public debate the freedom of the city was presented to Charles Stewart Parnell, a Protestant landowner from County Wicklow who had espoused the cause of Irish nationalism at Westminster. A public plebiscite had voted dramatically against the award but when the Town Council met, the vote was 22 for and 16 against the proposal. The Lord Provost, Sir John Boyd, boycotted the ceremony which was performed in a disgracefully slipshod fashion, but during his visit to the city Parnell spoke on the Irish home rule issue at several well-attended meetings in the city. Parnell's own popularity was eclipsed in November 1890 by the revelation of his adulterous relationship with Kitty O'Shea and his name was struck off the honorary burgess' role.

## 20th

**1938:** While serving as Governor-General of Canada, Lord Tweedsmuir of Elsfield was installed as Chancellor of the University of Edinburgh. Better known as the novelist John Buchan, the creator of the thriller *The Thirty-Nine Steps*, he had been Canada's Governor-General since 1935 and this was his first visit home to his native Scotland. Buchan had divided his childhood between Glasgow where his father was a minister, and the family home in the Borders, and although the course of his life had led him to the glittering prizes of successful careers as author, politician, diplomat and publisher, Scotland remained dear to his heart. Buchan had previously spent time in Edinburgh as a publisher before the First World War and as High Commissioner to the General Assembly in 1933.

## 21st

**1883:** The fifth Earl of Rosebery, whose family seat is at Dalmeny, near South Queensferry, was made a freeman of the city of Edinburgh. Later he was to become Foreign Secretary in Gladstone's government and between 1894 and 1895 he was Prime Minister. An eloquent and witty speaker, he was also an enthusiastic supporter of schemes to promote an understanding of Edinburgh's past and he was responsible for the restoration of Lady Stair's house on the Mound. In his speech of acceptance he remarked on his family's long connection with Edinburgh and added, "The faces around me are not strange; they are faces of old friends. I could have found my way blindfold today along that road which I traversed from my home to this hall. I know every house and every tree upon it. Everything is familiar. . . ."

# July

22nd _____

23rd _____

24th _____

# July

## 22nd

**1661:** King James VI was one of the first, but certainly not the last Scot in a position of authority to take an undue interest in witchcraft. Throughout his reign and continuing well into the seventeenth century, countless innocent, though no doubt rather strange and retiring women were tried and condemned to an agonising death for the crime of dabbling with black magic. One such was Janet Allan who, according to a contemporary Town Council minute, suffered in the Canongate along with her fellow accused Barbara Mylne "as one whom the said Jonet did once sie come in at the Wattergate in liknes of a catt and did chainge her garment under her awen staire and went in to her hous". This hideous practice had begun to die out in Edinburgh by the latter quarter of the century.

## 23rd

**1637:** When the Dean of Edinburgh attempted to use the new Service Book prescribed by King Charles I at Sunday service in the High Church of St Giles a serious riot broke out amongst the congregation. Tradition has it that a local woman, Jenny Geddes, threw the first stool at the unfortunate Dean and in the midst of the ensuing uproar as stools rained around him the Bishop of Edinburgh climbed into the pulpit in an unsuccessful attempt to restore order. The protestors were bundled outside the church and the service, according to the new liturgy, was completed behind closed doors. When the Bishop and the Dean reappeared they were stoned by the furious mob and it was only due to the quick thinking of the passing Earl of Roxburgh, who was able to save them, that no blood was shed that day.

## 24th

**1593:** One of the most frightening incidents in James VI's relationship with his cousin Francis Stewart, the Earl of Bothwell, took place in the early hours of the morning when Bothwell found a means of secretly stealing into the King's bedchamber. There he put his sovereign in a state of alarm — and James had good reason to be scared, two years before he had been held hostage in the same room by his madcap relative — but Bothwell had merely come to beg his pardon. For a while the two men were reconciled, but in 1595 his outrageous behaviour forced James to forfeit the Bothwell Border lands and the "Wizard Earl", as he was known popularly, fled to Naples where he died in 1612. Bothwell's behaviour often verged on lunacy and he is reputed to have been part of the plot hatched by the North Berwick witches.

# July

25th _____

26th _____

27th _____

# July

25th _____

**1883:** A letter from the Garter-at-Arms finally resolved the difficulty of Edinburgh's precedence at Royal occasions. A controversy had raged for several years about whether the Lord Provost of Edinburgh or the Lord Mayor of Dublin should be second in line to the Lord Mayor of London. The arguments between the two cities read today like a Victorian drawing-room melodrama and at one stage the Town Council prepared an eighty-page document which not only listed Edinburgh's historical and constitutional right to precedence but also haughtily denigrated Dublin and its pretensions. Edinburgh was finally, by the official letter, granted precedence over Dublin but the whole matter became academic after the independence of Ireland following the First World War.

26th _____

**1952:** The monument to the Royal Scots, "a story in stone and bronze which must remain unfinished as long as the regiment exists to add new chapters to it", according to *The Scotsman*'s report of the ceremony, "was unveiled on Saturday afternoon by the Colonel-in-Chief, Her Royal Highness the Princess Royal, who thereafter gave the Monument into the keeping of the Corporation of Edinburgh, 'to guard and maintain in perpetuity'. Over four thousand past and present soldiers of the First of Foot, the oldest regiment in the British army, watched the unveiling and later marched past while Her Royal Highness took the salute from the steps of the Royal Scottish Academy. Thousands of people, including many mothers and daughters, looked on as the battalions old and young passed along Princes Street."

27th _____

**1920:** Craiglockhart Hospital was finally purchased by the nuns of the Convent of the Sacred Heart after lengthy negotiations, thus allowing the foundation of a Catholic teachers' training college in Edinburgh. The imposing building on Craiglockhart Hill had started life as a hydropathic hotel in 1880 and it offered splendid bathing facilities as well as croquet lawns and pleasant walks on the surrounding hill. However, the hotel never prospered and it changed hands several times before it was used during the First World War as a hospital for officers recuperating from wounds received on the western front, as well as a psychiatric centre for those suffering from shellshock. Much of the imposing charm of the original building has been retained in the college.

# July

28th _____

29th _____

30th _____

# July

## 28th

**1587:** An early owner of the Barony of Broughton was Sir Lewis Bellenden who was granted it by charter under the Great Seal of King James VI "to be holden of his Majestie and his successors, in free heritage and free barony for ever, for yearly payment of the sum of two hundred pounds, Scots money . . . to be called in all time coming, the Barony of Broughton . . .". The Barony occupied the lands around the present-day Broughton Street and the territory to the west of the upper part of Leith Walk, and it remained an independent burgh until its amalgamation with Edinburgh after the jurisdictive powers of its Baron Bailies were removed in 1748. During its heyday Broughton boasted a tolbooth and jail and the Baron Bailies exercised their privilege of pit and gallows to execute prisoners whom they had tried.

## 29th

**1968:** The Director of the Military Tattoo, which is held at the Castle Esplanade during each Festival, announced that the massed pipes and drums of eight of the nine regiments of the Scottish Division would be appearing for the first time. "A total of 240 men will be included in the mass pipes and drums. This is the most that have ever been in this section of the Tattoo — and are ever likely to." Also taking part that year were a group of thirty-six cadets from Rutgers University, New Brunswick, New Jersey, who gave a thrilling display of precision drilling with sharply bayoneted rifles. The Brigade of Gurkhas made an appearance and to mark their fiftieth anniversary the Royal Air Force mounted a tableaux of their history which included three aircraft.

## 30th

**1850:** The novelist Charlotte Bronte, visiting Edinburgh, wrote to W. Smith Williams: ". . . and who indeed that has once seen Edinburgh, with its couchant crag-lion, but must see it again in dreams, waking or sleeping? My dear Sir, do not think I blaspheme when I tell you that your great London as compared to Dun-Edin, 'mine own romantic town', is as prose compared to poetry, or as a great rumbling, rambling, heavy epic compared to a lyric, brief, bright, clear, and vital as a flash of lightning. You have nothing like Scott's monument, or if you had that, and all the glories of architecture assembled together, you have nothing like Arthur's Seat, and above all you have not the Scotch national character after all which gives the land its true charm, its true greatness."

# July

**1863:** John Steell, R.S.A., made his first public announcement on the progress of the statue for Princes Street Gardens of Professor John Wilson who was better known in Edinburgh as "Christopher North". The statue was eventually unveiled in May 1864 and it reflected Wilson's ordinary careless ease of dress: the figure is covered by a plaid, leaning against the stump of a palm tree and with half-opened manuscript in his hands. "Christopher North" was one of the most remarkable characters in Edinburgh's literary history. He had made and broken reputations through his reckless editorial control of *Blackwood's Magazine* and he led several slashing attacks on the leading literary men of his day. A High-Tory, and something of a bully, he was for a time Professor of Moral Philosophy at the University.

# August

*Edinburgh is taken hostage by the Edinburgh International Festival and Fringe which both provide an almost bewildering array of theatre, opera, concerts and exhibitions. The festivals were founded in 1947.*

# August

1st ———————————————————

2nd ———————————————————

3rd ———————————————————

# August

## 1st

**1647:** Lammas, one of the Scottish quarter days, was the ancient Celtic festival of autumn and was celebrated by the sacrifice of the fruits of the soil to a god whom the Gaels called Iughaidh Lamhfhada. All over Scotland special fairs and horse races were held, and it was also a period of "handfasting" or trial marriages which lasted a year and a day. In country areas there were saining rites for the cattle, and Lammas fires, similar to those held at Beltane, or the first day of May, were popular well into the nineteenth century as was the baking of the Lammas bannock in a ceremony called the Fatling of Mary. In Edinburgh the festival was marked by driving horses down to the sea, a practice frowned upon by the Kirk Session: "that non goe to Leith . . . nor tak their horses to be washed in the sea".

## 2nd

**1530:** A local man called David Duly who knew that his wife was infected by plague, broke all the city's anti-plague laws by hearing mass in the High Church of St Giles and by so doing he "infekkit all the toun". The punishment was severe. A gibbet was hurriedly constructed against the front door of his house but the rope broke and "at the will of God he has escapit". Amongst the punishments for harbouring those infected by plague, the following expedients are mentioned in Town Council records: fines, imprisonment, banishment from the town, the stocks, the ducking stool, the jougs or pillory, whipping, branding, nailing by the ear to the tron or weighbridge, hanging and drowning. Despite those grim penalties, plague was not to be stamped out from the city for many years.

## 3rd

**1796:** The Town Council agreed to award a sum of fifteen guineas to the Edinburgh Burgess Golfing Society for the improvement of the links at Bruntsfield which lie to the west of the Meadows. Golf had been played over the links since the beginning of the sixteenth century but quarrying operations had left them in a wretched condition. In 1717 James Brownhill, a burgess and brewer of the city, built a tavern near the links called Golfhall and there is a "nineteenth hole" on the links to this day — although it is doubtfu whether its claims to be five hundred years old are at all possible. The game of golf and the business of quarrying continued to interfere with each other and it was not until the beginning of the nineteenth century that the game's rights were protected. there is a pitch and putt course on the site today.

# August

4th _____

5th _____

6th _____

## 4th

**1870:** In a small house in Portobello — generally thought to have been the cottage at the corner of the High Street and Bridge Street — the comedian Harry Lauder was born, the son of a potter. After working for a time as a coalminer, Lauder became a music hall singer and comedian and went on to become one of the most popular entertainers of his day with songs like "Roamin' in the Gloamin' ", "Keep Right on to the End of the Road" and "I Love a Lassie". Although he was one of the best known men of his day, a super-star of stage and screen and a wealthy man who was knighted for his efforts, Lauder's public persona of a bewhiskered, kilted half-wit, drunk or sober, who sang daft, sentimental songs, did much harm, producing to the world at large a harmful stereotype of the Scot.

## 5th

**1651:** Scotland's first newspaper, *Mercurius Scoticus*, was published, and although neither the place where it was printed nor the printer's name were mentioned, it is generally supposed to have been printed in Leith. It was to be published weekly and its eight pages consisted mainly of a digest of news gleaned from London. By November in the following year it had given way to a newspaper which was published in London but reprinted in Leith, *A Diurnall of Some Passages and Affairs*, but it too was short-lived and was superseded by *Mercurius Politicus*. A printer in Leith continued to handle the new paper's Scottish reprinting until 1655 when it was reprinted in Edinburgh and that year marks the first occasion when a newspaper was put to press in Scotland's capital.

## 6th

**1729:** One of Edinburgh's greatest Lord Provosts, George Drummond, who did so much to ensure that the Georgian New Town was built, opened a new infirmary in a small house that was soon to move, by Royal Charter, to a building in Infirmary Street between the Cowgate and what is now the South Bridge. The Royal Infirmary was to remain there until 1870 when it moved into its present headquarters at Lauriston overlooking the Meadows. Today it is one of the most famous and best-equipped teaching hospitals in the world with a reputation both for its medical care and for its interests in the furtherance of clinical and surgical research. Through connections with the medical departments of the University, the Royal Infirmary has been involved in most of the major medical innovations associated with the city.

# August

7th _____

8th _____

9th _____

# August

## 7th

**1751:** St Mary's Street, which links the High Street to the Cowgate near the point where the Netherbow once stood, takes its name from the chapel and hospital dedicated to the Virgin Mary which, according to the protocol book of William Forbes, stood at the head of the wynd on the west side. These buildings were destroyed in 1572 and they were frequently confused with the neighbouring convent of St Mary of Placentia which lay to the other, southern, side of the Cowgate and to which legend has it, the Pleasance of today is supposed to owe its name. St Mary's Street has been long neglected by the city and its nineteenth-century tenement buildings are in need of much care and attention. It also suffers from being a main route from the city to the southern suburbs.

## 8th

**1503:** The marriage between James IV and Princess Margaret of the English Royal House of Tudor was celebrated in the Abbey of Holyrood. Before the ceremony James received his English guests with much pomp and circumstance in the great hall of the palace and set the Archbishop of York on his right hand. The marriage was performed by the Archbishop of Glasgow and the English churchman read the papal bull consenting to the union. After Mass the party proceeded back to the palace for a great banquet and a variety of sumptuous entertainments which astonished the English visitors who had long held to the mistaken belief that Scotland was a poor, backward, unsophisticated nation. Jousts were held in the park by the palace and the celebrations continued for another seven days.

## 9th

**1693:** The observation of the Lord's Day has been an integral part of Edinburgh life since the Reformation, although as a Town Council edict from the end of the seventeenth century makes clear, the city fathers frequently had to remind the citizens of their obligations: "They strictly prohibit and discharge all persones whatsomever within this City or suburbs thereof to brew or work any other handy work or labour on the Lords day or to be found on the streets standing or walking idle or to goe in company or vage to the Castlehill publick yeards or feilds on that day at any tyme thereof and discharges all persones to goe to ail houses or tavernes for eating and drinking the tyme of sermon or unseasonably or necessaryly at any tyme on the Lords day." The warning was repeated again in following years.

# August

10th _____


11th _____


12th _____

# August

## 10th

**1807:** Nine months after William Begbie, the porter of the British Linen Bank, had been murdered and robbed in Tweeddale Court, a journeyman mason and his two companions discovered in the grounds of Bellevue a parcel containing £3,000 of the £5,000 that had been stolen. The bank rewarded the three men with £200 but the identity of the murderer remained a mystery. Only one person had witnessed the crime — a boy sailor home on leave saw a tall man with a yellow paper parcel running out of Tweeddale Court. Sixteen years later the boy had become a teacher and on his return to Edinburgh he gave his evidence to the police who were then hunting a daring black-coated man who had been terrorising Scotland with his bank robberies. In 1820 a man called Mackoull was arrested for the Begbie murder and other bank robberies.

## 11th

**1931:** The social reformer Patrick Geddes, in his seventy-seventh year, gave his one and only radio broadcast from the Edinburgh studios of B.B.C. Radio. His subject was "When Scotland Awakes" and he took as his theme the need for decentralisation from London as opposed to complete separation. Geddes had lived in Edinburgh during the eighteen-eighties and he was responsible for the picturesque construction of the houses of Ramsay Garden by the Castle esplanade and for the reconstruction of the camera obscura in Outlook Tower which had been the town house of the Laird o' Cockpen. He had been involved, too, in the efforts of the Edinburgh Social Union to better the abysmal living conditions that then prevailed in the Royal Mile and he was an early supporter of town and country planning.

## 12th

**1832:** The passing of the Reform Bill on 7th June was the great event of the year and the triumphant conclusion to Earl Grey's proposals was celebrated in Edinburgh, as in many other British cities. A monster procession was organised in the city by the Trades Council and it marched through the city from Bruntsfield Links, along Princes Street, to Leith, before returning to its starting point by way of the Canongate and the old town. To prevent any doubts among the Tories of Edinburgh that this was a subversive display, great care was taken to sing only patriotic songs and during the course of the day a number of loyal resolutions were passed by the crowd. The first elections occasioned by the Bill took place on 17th December when the Lord Advocate Francis Jeffrey was elected member for Edinburgh.

# August

13th ————————————————————————

14th ————————————————————————

15th ————————————————————————

# August

## 13th

**1701:** Ten o'clock at night was set by the Town Council as the closing time for all Edinburgh taverns, following a saturnalian outburst of drinking by some of the city's inhabitants. "The Councill considering that the suffering of persones to drink unseasonablie in Tavernes cellars and such other places and not oblidging all persones to repair tymeously to their lodgings at night is one of the greatest causes of the abounding of drunkennes, uncleannes, night revellings and other Immoralities and disorders both in houses and upon the streets and is a great hinderance to sober persones in their worshipping of God in secret and in their families. . . ." Public houses in Edinburgh can now open from eleven o'clock in the morning until eleven o'clock or later at night.

## 14th

**1773:** Dr Samuel Johnson arrived in Edinburgh and according to his biographer James Boswell, he "had for many years given me hopes that we should go together and visit the Hebrides . . . in spring 1773 he talked of coming to Scotland that year . . . on Saturday late in the evening I received a note from him, that he was arrived at Boyd's Inn at the head of the Canongate. I went to him directly. He embraced me cordially . . . Dr Johnson and I walked arm-in-arm up the High Street to my house in James' Court; it was a dusky night; I could not prevent his being assailed by the evening effluvia of Edinburgh . . . my wife had tea ready for him, which it well known he delighted to drink at all hours . . . he showed much complacency upon finding that the mistress of the house was so attentive to his singular habit."

## 15th

**1771:** The novelist Sir Walter Scott was born in a house at the top of College Wynd, an unhealthy, stinking warren of tall houses so closely packed together that neighbours in the top flats could shake hands across the narrow street that led to the Cowgate. It has long since disappeared, but the modern dog-legged Guthrie Street, which connects Chambers Street to the Cowgate, gives some idea of its whereabouts. Scott's father was a lawyer and his mother was the daughter of the University's Professor of Medicine, John Rutherford. Scott himself followed the legal profession and became a clerk to the Court of Session, but he is best known internationally as a novelist of power and imagination, the creator of the "Waverley" novels, and of long romantic poems like "The Lady of the Lake".

# August

16th _____

17th _____

18th _____

# August

## 16th

**1676:** Although its origins are lost in the mists of antiquity, the first recorded meeting of the Royal Company of Archers took place shortly after its rules had been formalised by a governing council. The rules of the Royal Company of Archers allowed for the establishment of an annual wappinschaw or shooting competition with a goose as the target, but this barbaric practice ceased in the nineteenth century. The Company's most ancient prize is the Silver Arrow which is shot for annually on Musselburgh Links. With their colourful green uniforms and feathered bonnets the archers play a distinctive part in Edinburgh's pageantry and they have the honour of being the sovereign's official bodyguard in Scotland. Their membership is drawn mainly from the Scottish aristocracy.

## 17th

**1846:** After the death of Sir Walter Scott in 1832 his son-in-law, John Gibson Lockhart, suggested that the city should raise a memorial to one of its greatest sons. A committee was formed and it decided to build a monument on the south side of Princes Street with funds being raised by subscription and through public concerts and other events. George Kemp, a self-taught draughtsman, was engaged to execute the design of this unforgettable spikey monument to Scott's genius. As the years wore on the construction was hampered by lack of funds and Kemp himself was drowned accidentally in the Union Canal two years before his monument was opened officially by the Lord Provost. The statues representing characters from Scott's novels were added in 1880.

## 18th

**1650:** In the quiet village of Colinton, now a suburb of Edinburgh, ten companies of General Monck's regiment took up their quarters during Cromwell's siege of Edinburgh Castle. Its commander, Colonel Walter Dundas of Dundas, eventually surrendered the Castle on Christmas Eve but by then the parliamentary army had caused a great deal of damage to the city. Colinton village, in spite of the encroaching army of modern housing developments, remains a peaceful backwater with its church and manse, once the home of Robert Louis Stevenson's maternal grandparents. There is a grand walk back towards Edinburgh by the Water of Leith as it meanders through Colinton Dell which has several ruined eighteenth-century mills within its shaded wood. Nearby is Bonaly Tower, once the home of Lord Cockburn.

# August

19th _____

20th _____

21st _____

# August

## 19th

**1561:** Mary, Queen of Scots, set foot on her native soil after an absence of thirteen years when her ship landed at the port of Leith from France. Her arrival had been delayed by several days of unseasonal fog in the Firth of Forth, but by nine o'clock in the morning a warm sun beat down from a cloudless sky and boded well for her reign. As Holyroodhouse was unprepared for her arrival at such an early time of day, she spent the morning in the house of Andrew Lamb in Leith where she met her principal supporters amongst the nobility. Later that night, the people of Edinburgh serenaded her outside the palace with a coarse mixture of ballads and psalms that a contemporary description found to be "so ill and in such bad accord that there could be nothing worse".

## 20th

**1962:** "The Scottish literary world put on a little domestic comedy for the benefit of visitors to the International Writers' Conference in the McEwan Hall. It was the familiar kitchen scene where the protagonists throw crockery at each other, where the father figure speaks of tradition, adolescent son flounces out to play Teddy Boys in the street instead of joining the family liturgy, and the neighbours look on in some embarrassment . . . the 'Scottish Day' as expected turned into a squabble between the traditional nationalists and the internationalists. There was some entertaining flare-ups. Alexander Trocchi . . . purged himself of a few disgusts, he called the discussion, 'turgid, petty, provincial, stale, cold-porridge, Bible-clasping nonsense. Of what is interesting in the last 20 years of Scottish writing I have written it all'." Magnus Magnusson in *The Scotsman*.

## 21st

**1949:** The third Edinburgh International Film Festival was opened by three of the world's greatest documentary film-makers, John Grierson, Robert Flaherty and Sir Stephen Tallents, the only occasion that all three men shared the same platform together. Following eloquent speeches by Grierson and Tallents on the need for documentary films that "would touch not only the minds but also the imaginations of men", Flaherty rose to speak but sensing that words would not be called for, he bowed and thanked the audience for their enthusiastic response to his film *Louisiana Story* which had been shown the previous year. It was an early highlight in the festival which had been founded to concentrate on the art of the documentary. By the late nineteen-sixties the festival had emerged as one of the world's leading film festivals.

# August

22nd _____

23rd _____

24th _____

# August

## 22nd

**1822:** During his triumphant visit to his northern capital, King George IV spent his seventh day in a grand procession from Holyroodhouse to the Castle. The city had gone tartan-mad for the occasion and the King's party was escorted by platoons of Highlanders and by a squadron of cavalry of the Royal Scots Greys. Over 300,000 spectators were said to have crammed themselves into the Royal Mile to watch the triumphant procession and in the evening a ball in the King's honour was held by the peerage of Scotland in the Assembly Rooms in George Street. A permanent memento of the visit is enshrined in the tablet where the Royal party landed on the foreshore in Leith, marked O FELICEM DIEM! Much of the elaborate arrangements for the visit had been planned by Sir Walter Scott.

## 23rd

**1900:** During a routine training exercise at the fire station in Lauriston Place, one of the firemen, James Hetherill, "was being carried down a ladder by another fireman, when he slipped off the latter's shoulders, and fell a considerable distance, alighting on his head. He was removed to the Chalmers Hospital across the street but died soon after admittance." *The Scotsman*'s report was accompanied by a photograph of the kind of realistic and strenuous exercises carried out at the brigade's new headquarters which had been opened two months previously. Under their Firemaster Arthur Pordage, the Edinburgh Fire Brigade also increased its strength to sixty-two horse-drawn engines and in 1906 it acquired the first of its Merryweather motorised fire engines, the most powerful machine of its day.

## 24th

**1947:** The first Edinburgh International Festival opened to acclaim from all sides and *The Scotsman* reported not only an increase of jollity within the city but also the bonus of summer sunshine. "Edinburgh has surprised even some of her citizens by the manner in which she has adapted herself to the new role of Festival City. The spirit evoked in many directions has been a contributory factor in the success which has marked the opening days of the venture. Visitors have been able to sense a friendly stimulating atmosphere and the variety of the attractions additional to the official programme has attracted both gratifying evidence of a will to co-operate and opportunities of enjoyment for those whose have time to make the most of the occasion." The Festival was opened by the Duke and Duchess of Gloucester.

# August

25th _____

26th _____

27th _____

# August

## 25th

**1776:** The distinguished Scottish philosopher David Hume died in Edinburgh, the city he had come to regard as his home. Born and brought up in Berwickshire, Hume had studied law at the University, but finding it "nauseous" he had lived for a time in France. During his time in Edinburgh he lived at Riddle's Land on the south side of the Lawnmarket, then moved to Jack's Land in the Canongate before moving to James Court on the north side of the Lawnmarket. His last residence was the house he had built for himself in St David Street and his James Court residence was leased to James Boswell who visited him as he was dying and went away amazed at Hume's stoic acceptance of his fate. Hume's best-known works are *Treatise on Human Nature* (1739) and *Essays Moral and Political* (1741).

## 26th

**1881:** A force of 40,000 Scottish Volunteers — the largest group of men at arms to have assembled in the city since King James IV marched to disaster at the Battle of Flodden — was reviewed in Holyrood Park by Queen Victoria. The whole force was under the command of Major-General Alastair MacDonald and a large crowd had turned up to view the parade which included a goodly number of military and pipe bands. But, as so often happens in Edinburgh during the summer, the event was ruined by an unseasonable downpour of rain that gradually drove away the expectant spectators, although *The Scotsman* noted that "the Queen remained to the last, and so did the rest of the Royal party". The Queen later reported her "entire satisfaction with the appearance of the troops assembled".

## 27th

**1817:** During his visit to meet Sir Walter Scott, the American historian Washington Irving wrote about his impressions of Edinburgh in a letter to his New York relations. "It seemed as if the rock and castle assumed a new aspect every time I looked at them; and Arthur's Seat was perfect witchcraft. I don't wonder that anyone residing in Edinburgh should write poetically; I rambled about the bridges and on Calton height yesterday, in a perfect intoxication of the mind. I did not visit a single public building; but merely gazed and revelled on the romantic scenery about me. The enjoyment of yesterday alone would be a sufficient compensation for the whole journey. . . ." Earlier in the letter he had complained somewhat bitterly, but no doubt accurately, about the "steady, pitiless rain".

# August

28th _____




29th _____




30th _____

# August

## 28th

**1966:** "All that has been said about the new (and very welcome) Richard Demarco Gallery at 8 Melville Crescent," wrote Sydney Goodsir Smith in *The Scotsman*, "is perfectly true. Lavish is the word. Lavish catalogue with colour illustrations, lavish collection of paintings with great names — far too many of them to list — more than 60 of them. At first it seems a bit too much but it isn't really. This is a miniature Gallery of Modern Art, international art. . . ." Richard Demarco had been one of the founding members of the Traverse Theatre Club and during his stay at Melville Crescent his gallery put on at times bewildering arrays of exhibitions from all over the world. Later the gallery moved into the High Street where Demarco evolved the astonishingly successful Edinburgh Arts Journeys.

## 29th

**1805:** The undeveloped area to the south of the city known as Newington was purchased by Dr Benjamin Bell, an eminent surgeon and the great-grandfather of the future model for Conan Doyle's Sherlock Holmes, Dr Joseph Bell. Newington began to be developed during the nineteenth century, partly because people began to want to live in country seclusion and also because the construction of the South Bridge and of Minto Street afforded easier access to the city centre. Bell's son sold the lands to Sir George Stewart of Grantully who developed the quiet preserve of the Blacket estate which is still a haven of quiet streets and elegant town houses in the middle of a busy suburb. Newington House, which was built in 1805, had a variety of distinguished owners and was demolished in 1966.

## 30th

**1678:** "The Councill upon report to the thesaurer anent the repairing of the stair of the tolbuith of the Cannongate Doe grant warrand to the thesaurer to caus repair of the said stair and for that effect to agrie with a masson at als easie an rait as he can." Built in 1591 the Canongate Tolbooth may well have been in need of repair, but the Council's caution over expenses should not be interpreted as meanness towards a venerable building — it was, after all, one of the city's jails and remained so until 1818. In its day it had also served as a council house and courtroom and it bears the stag's head and cross, the coat of arms of the burgh of the Canongate. The large clock was added in 1820 and today the building acts as one of the city's museums.

# August
31st_____

**1842:** One of the most mismanaged Royal visits in the city's history had its origins in a misty August evening when Queen Victoria's Royal yacht accompanied by a squadron of warships slipped into the Firth of Forth. Due to a series of misunderstandings, the Queen and Prince Albert landed unheralded at Leith at eight o'clock the following morning and when Victoria arrived at Inverleith to receive the keys of the city from the Lord Provost, Sir James Forrest, neither he nor the Town Council were there to meet her. There was little the Royal party could do but to proceed to Dalkeith palace where they were the guests of the Duke of Buccleuch. But the dismayed members of the Town Council stole a march on the Royal party and just managed to arrive at the gates of the palace to welcome the Queen and to offer apologies.

# September

The Palace of Holyroodhouse, Edinburgh's Royal residence, was built originally as a guest-house for its neighbouring, though now ruined, Abbey. Sacked several times by invading armies it owes its present austere shape to Sir William Bruce.

# September

1st _____

2nd _____

3rd _____

# September

## 1st

**1557:** On the Feast of St Giles a group of Reformers stole the effigy of the saint from the church in the High Street and tossed it into the Nor' Loch. The festival had been a popular event in the city's calendar: the church was decorated with flowers and evergreens and the effigy of the saint was paraded down the High Street with a great display of pageantry and music. Somewhat bizarrely, in the van of the parade the city's butchers led a prize bull which had been decorated with embroidery and adorned with a laurel crown. Eventually the festival had fallen into disrepute and the revels were frowned upon by the Reformers who took over the church in 1560 for their own use. An important relic had been the armbone of St Giles, a sixth-century saint of Greek origin.

## 2nd

**1908:** Christopher Murray Grieve, who was to make his poetic nom de plume of Hugh MacDiarmid famous the world over, was appointed as a pupil-teacher to Broughton Higher Grade School in Macdonald Road. While he was there his English teacher, George Ogilvie, remarked on Grieve's sharp intellect and on his easy ability with language. Grieve left Edinburgh in 1910 to return to his native Borders but was to return frequently in later life when his favourite pub was Milne's Bar, that haunt of poets in Hanover Street. An ardent nationalist, and a believer in the unity of international socialism, Hugh MacDiarmid is perhaps best known for the publication in 1926 of his great poem *A Drunk Man Looks at the Thistle*, for his *Three Hymns to Lenin* and for the beautiful intensity of his early lyrics.

## 3rd

**1947:** After a lengthy and at times acrimonious battle with Emmanuel Shinwell, the Minister of Fuel and Power, Edinburgh was allowed to floodlight the Castle for the first time since the end of the Second World War. "If two sounds stood out above those which are normally heard in Princes Street of an evening," wrote the noon edition of the *Evening Dispatch* (price three halfpence), "they were gasps of amazement and comments of praise one heard coming from groups of people — some in evening gowns — standing gazing skywards, and the even more continual sound of cameras being mounted on tripods and being moved for better angle shots." The first rain of the Festival had threatened the spectacle but a clear dark night had added to the beauty of the scene.

# September

4th _____

5th _____

6th _____

# September

## 4th

**1964:** The last crossing by the ferry boat *Queen Margaret* was made between North and South Queensferry when the Forth Road Bridge was opened by H.M. The Queen. The coat of arms of the burgh of South Queensferry proclaimed its ancient right to ferry travellers across the narrows of the Forth estuary, a right gained from the frequent journeyings between Edinburgh and Dunfermline of St Margaret and her husband, King Malcolm Canmore, in the eleventh century. Queensferry's link with that long past came to an end when the elegant suspension bridge carrying the motorway north was opened on a day of early morning mist that threatened the ceremony. As the hour approached for the Queen to drive across, the sun shone through the mist and the bridge came dramatically into full view, 500 feet above the river.

## 5th

**1750:** In a house in Cap and Feather Close (long disappeared below the North Bridge) was born the poet Robert Fergusson, who was destined to die at the early age of twenty-four in the Edinburgh Bedlam. He was educated in Dundee and St Andrews but he returned to Edinburgh to work as a lowly clerk in the Commissary Office. Through all his poetry shines the spirit of Edinburgh and his long poem *Auld Reekie* is a loving hymn of praise to the dirty, rumbustious, licentious world of tavern and club where drink and social equality reigned supreme. All of Edinburgh, its oyster cellars, the races on Leith Links, the City Guard, and the city's festivities were grist to his mill and Fergusson remains Auld Reekie's poet *par excellence*. He lies buried in the Canongate churchyard.

## 6th

**1646:** Three years before his death, the poet William Drummond of Hawthornden, admitted to his diary that old age was taking a toll on his health and well-keeping: "I contracted a goute which removed from one parte to another." The entries for his latter years make constant reference to sickness of one kind or another, "goute", "a sort of Tootheach", "an apoplexie", "a cold and fievre" and in his remote house of Hawthornden on the banks of the River North Esk to the south of the city near Lasswade, Drummond lived out his melancholic, reclusive final years. As a young man he had acted as a kind of poet laureate to Edinburgh and his wide learning and schooling in European culture earned him the respect of poets and scholars elsewhere, including Ben Jonson who visited him in 1618.

# September

7th _____

8th _____

9th _____

# September

## 7th

**1736:** Following a riot earlier that year at the execution of Andrew Wilson, a smuggler, Captain John Porteous had ordered his City Guard to fire on an angry crowd and eight people were killed. Porteous himself was sentenced to hang but, due to his influence with Queen Caroline, he was subsequently reprieved, much to the fury of the Edinburgh mob who decided to take the law into their own hands. The door of the Tolbooth was burned down and the wretched Porteous was dragged to the Grassmarket where he was hanged on a dyer's pole. The conspirators were never discovered and the government's fury at the outrage was centred on the city council which was fined £2,000 the following year. There is a graphic description of the riot in Scott's novel *The Heart of Midlothian.*

## 8th

**1662:** One of the most prominent men to take part in the Pentland Rising of 1666, Hugh McKail, preached his last sermon in Moredun, near Liberton, before the Act banning nonconformist ministers became law. A party of dragoons moved out to Moredun to arrest him but he was able to escape to his father's property at Bothwell and evaded arrest until the day of the Battle of Rullion Green four years later. Unable, because of sickness, to keep up with the Covenanting army, McKail was arrested on the Braid Hills and taken to the Tolbooth where he was tortured by the "boot", an instrument that shattered his leg in eleven places. He refused to confess his nonconformism and was hanged in a state of religious exaltation with other survivors from the battle at a gallows in the Grassmarket.

## 9th

**1892:** Four days after it opened its doors to pupils the South Morningside School recorded its popularity in south Edinburgh: "Unexpectedly large numbers of 572. Many of these, especially amongst infants and younger juveniles, have come from numerous private schools in the district kept by ladies. This factor increases the difficulty of proper classification throughout the school. The other schools which have contributed most largely to our roll are the old Morningside School (which is now closed), Gorgie Public School and Gillespie's." The school was opened formally with much pomp and ceremony a month later and amongst the distinguished guests were the philanthropist Andrew Carnegie and Professor David Masson, a pioneer of higher education and supporter of the idea of universal education.

# September

10th _____

11th _____

12th _____

# September

10th _____

**1883:** The Royal Lyceum Theatre opened with a performance of *Much Ado About Nothing*, with Henry Irving as Benedick and Ellen Terry as Beatrice attracting a packed house on the first night. William Fowler who was to become Registrar for Selkirk was the first paying customer and fifty years later, in the jubilee programme, he was to remember the glittering occasion not so much for the performance — he could only afford a seat in the gods — but for "the enthusiasm and applause on the part of the audience". The Lyceum, which was owned by the theatrical management of Howard and Wyndham, enjoyed several successes during its first fifty years including a run of plays by George Bernard Shaw and a performance of Barrie's *The Admirable Crichton* in 1931 before King George V.

11th _____

**1782:** Reid's Close in the Canongate takes its name from Andrew Reid, a bailie of the Canongate, who owned malt barns in the vicinity. The lands to the east were owned by the Duke of Queensberry and to the west by Andrew's brother Robert. After the Reids' death their lands were bought by the guild of weavers of the Canongate although the family name continued to be used for the close and its lands. Reid's Close shared a common entry with the access to Haddington Court which was the town house of the Earl of Haddington built in the late seventeenth or early eighteenth century. A charter granted by the burgh of the Canongate passed the ownership of the yards and gardens from William Wilson of Soonhope, a lawyer, to the Haddington family and the close was known for a time as Haddington's Close.

12th _____

**1423:** The Abbot of Holyrood, Dean John of Leith, gave the city five years' rental of the area of Canonmills together with its pertinents and rents. Canonmills had been granted to the monks of Holyrood by King David I in 1128 and it was also due to the generosity of the King that a large mill was built for the monks on the banks of the Water of Leith. Although the mills of the area, which lies to the north of the city at the edge of the New Town, are long closed, Canonmills is still not without its historical interest. In Tanfield Lane is a remnant of the Tanfield Hall, built in 1825, being the scene of a public dinner for the Irish patriot Daniel O'Connell in 1835 and, more famously perhaps, as the meeting place for the formation of the Free Church of Scotland at the time of the Disruption in 1843.

# September

13th _____

14th _____

15th _____

# September

## 13th

**1850:** The novelist Robert Lewis Balfour Stevenson (he later changed to the more familiar Louis) was born at 8 Howard Place in Stockbridge. He came from a long line of marine engineers and he himself studied engineering for a time at the University, but by the age of twenty, writing had captured him. The world remembers him as a novelist and poet, the creator of such memorable characters as Long John Silver in *Treasure Island* and Alan Breck Stewart and David Balfour in *Kidnapped*. Illness and a dislike of Edinburgh's long, damp, cold and windy winters eventually drove him for his otherwise beloved city to find refuge and a kinder climate in Samoa in the South Pacific where he died at the early age of forty-four.

## 14th

**1128:** One of the stories about the founding of the Abbey of Holyrood has its origins in a legend told about King David I, the son of St Margaret and King Malcolm Canmore. Ignoring the advice of his priests and churchmen, David set out on a Sunday to hunt on the slopes of Arthur's Seat within the Royal park. There he was attacked by a wondrous stag, "the farest hart that ever was sene afore with leavand creatour". It threw him to the ground and would have crushed him to death with its powerful antlers had not David reached up to save himself from their reach. In the middle of the vicious antlers a cross appeared and when the King grasped it the stag miraculously disappeared. The incident convinced David that he should build an Abbey of the Holy Rood (Cross) near the spot of the miracle.

## 15th

**1595:** The pupils of the town's High School, which was situated in the Yards, now Infirmary Street opposite the Old College, barricaded themselves in their school after being refused a statutory holiday. Despite the headmaster's pleas they stayed put and in desperation a deputation of town officers, led by Baillie John McMorran, was despatched to reason with the boys. However, they were in no mood for discussion and one boy from an influential Caithness family, William Sinclair, shot the Baillie in the head, killing him instantly. Such was the family's standing that Sinclair got off scot free and the powerless Town Council could only offer a weak reprimand to the headmaster, "to attend more diligently upon the school and scholars . . .".

# September

16th _____

17th _____

18th _____

# September

## 16th

**1803:** "We set out upon our walk, and went through many streets to Holyrood House, and thence to the hill called Arthur's Seat, a high hill, very rocky at the top, and below covered with smooth turf, on which sheep were feeding. We climbed up till we came to St Anthony's Well and Chapel, as it is called, but it is more like a hermitage than a chapel — a small ruin, which from its situation is exceedingly interesting, though in itself not remarkable . . . the castle rock looked exceedingly large through the misty air: a cloud of black smoke overhung the city, which combined with the rain and mist to conceal the shapes of the houses — an obscurity which added much to the grandeur of the sound that proceeded from it." Dorothy Wordsworth confided that description to her diary when she visited Edinburgh with her brother William.

## 17th

**1745:** At five o'clock in the morning the Highlanders of Cameron of Lochiel entered the city through the Netherbow and set about occupying Edinburgh. They were the advance guard of the Jacobite army of Prince Charles Edward Stewart, or Bonnie Prince Charlie as he is more popularly known, which had arrived in Corstorphine two days earlier. After some half-hearted opposition by the City Guard and some dragoons the city found itself in Highland hands by breakfast time that day. At twelve o'clock a manifesto proclaiming Charles as regent on behalf of his father James, the "Old Pretender", was read at the Mercat Cross. During their six-week stay in the capital the Highland army behaved with dignity but failed to capture the support of the population.

## 18th

**1834:** A public dinner was held in celebration of the granting of the freedom of the city to Earl Grey, the hero of the Reform Bill. Because no hall could be found to entertain the two-and-a-half thousand guests, a pavilion was hurriedly erected in the grounds of the Royal High School. Its interior was lit by a huge gas chandelier borrowed from the Theatre Royal and the scene was set for a glittering occasion in front of an excited, cheering crowd. Unfortunately, their enthusiasm overcame decorum and half the guests had started, and had indeed completed, their meals before Earl Grey had entered the pavilion and the speeches of welcome had been read. The most graphic description of the unhappy affair appeared in the *Morning Chronicle* whose reporter was the then unknown Charles Dickens.

# September

19th _____

20th _____

21st_____

# September

## 19th

**1815:** The foundation stone was laid for the construction of the Regent Bridge which was to connect the newly constructed Waterloo Place to the east end of Princes Street, thereby joining the Calton Hill to the ridge on which the New Town is chiefly built. According to a contemporary account there was an imposing Masonic and civic procession from the High Church of St Giles to the building site and it was "the most brilliant procession which ever adorned the annals of Masonry". Two thousand Masons were present at the occasion and although the weather was poor a large crowd had gathered to watch the ceremony. At the same time a new jail was begun on the south side of Calton Hill (now demolished) and a year later the prisoners from the Tolbooth were marched to their new place of confinement.

## 20th

**1824:** "A Railway on which wheel carriages are to be moved by steam engines seems a serious agitation as an improved mode of communication between Manchester & Liverpool. Our paper of this day notices a similar railway to be projected for connecting Edinburgh with Dalkeith & Musselburgh & that £36,000 raised by subscription on shares will answer the purpose." An anonymous writer of a journal of civic affairs commented on the beginnings of a railway mania that was soon to sweep the country. Obviously the writer took a great interest in the projected railway and may even have had shares in it such is his interest in its development in future years. By 1826 work had commenced on its construction, two years later the track was approaching Duddingston Loch and it was completed in 1831.

## 21st

**1730:** The *Caledonian Mercury* announced that David Beat had started offering his services as a writing master from his lodgings in Carrubber's Close off the High Street near the North Bridge of today. This historic close probably derives its name from one William de Carabris who lived there in the middle of the fifteenth century and it was there that John Spottiswoode, Archbishop of St Andrews had his town house in 1635 after becoming Lord Chancellor for Scotland. Other associations with the close include that of Allan Ramsay who opened a theatre there in 1736, but it enjoyed only a brief existence due to the opposition of the Town Council. It later became the Whitfield Chapel and the headquarters of the Carrubber's Close Mission, where a dispensary was run by Sir James Y. Simpson, the discoverer of chloroform as an anaesthetic.

# September

22nd ————————————————————————————

23rd ————————————————————————————

24th ————————————————————————————

# September

## 22nd

**1585:** The biblical names of the area of Morningside known as Edinburgh's "Bible Belt" — such as Canaan, Jordan, Goshen and Hebron — are reputed to have several origins, the most popular being that the lands were once occupied by gypsies. Certainly, Egypt is first mentioned in a Town Council record which states that Robert Fairlie had granted the city the use of his "houssis callit Littil Egypt besyde the commoun mure for the brewin thairin of the drink for the seik folkis of the mure". The drink was for the victims of an appalling outbreak of plague and they were housed in wooden shacks near the chapel of St Roque in what is now the grounds of the Astley Ainslie Hospital. The name Canaan first appeared in 1661 and for many years the neighbouring farm was called Egypt Farm.

## 23rd

**1960:** The departmental store chain, the House of Fraser, announced that it was to erect a musical clock at the corner of Hope Street and Princes Street in the West End of the city at a site that will always be known to generations of Edinburghers as Binns' Corner. The clock, which played a variety of tunes including "Scotland the Brave" and "Caller Herrin'", was fixed to the corner of Binns, the House of Fraser's West End store (now known more prosaically as Fraser's) and it was designed in the shape of a mock medieval castle. As the tune was played — before each quarter — a procession of pipers paraded around the base of the clock. A good deal of controversy surrounded the erection of the clock — especially and understandably from offices in the area, and its chimes are now a thing of the past.

## 24th

**1669:** John Lauder, a burgess of the city, took possession of an area in Newington which rejoiced in the somewhat unfortunate title of Lowsielaw, a name still commemorated by Lussielaw Street. Because the lands were on a raised knoll there is good reason to believe that the derivation is from the term "lossie" meaning "sparse" or "unprofitable". The word was used in several parts of Edinburgh, most notably in the southern part of the district of St Leonard's between Simon Square and the intersection of Crosscauseway with the Pleasance. A minor battle took place there in 1571 between soldiers from the Castle and men of the Regent's party but the whole area has enjoyed an unprofitable history, thus justifying its name perhaps and only in recent years have attempts been made to rejuvenate it.

# September

25th _____

26th _____

27th _____

# September

## 25th

**1965:** The former Morningside High Church, a handsome red sandstone building, was reopened as the Churchhill Theatre, a much needed addition to the city's theatre facilities. The opening ceremony was performed by Tom Fleming, one of Scotland's best known actors, and the first production was Oscar Wilde's *The Importance of Being Earnest* which was produced by the Scottish Community Drama Association. As well as being used all year round as a venue for amateur dramatic productions, the Churchhill Theatre has frequently been called into service during the Edinburgh International Festival as a venue for drama and ballet productions. Edinburgh enjoys a variety of amateur dramatic companies and the provision of this new theatre filled the gap left by the demolition of the Little Theatre in the Pleasance.

## 26th

**1753:** The poet Oliver Goldsmith spent some time in Edinburgh and in one of his graphic letters to Robert Bryanton of Ballymallon he described the dancing assemblies or balls that were then so popular. "When a stranger enters the dancing-hall he sees one end of the room taken up by the ladies, who sit dismally in a group by themselves — and in the other end stand their pensive partners that are to be — but no more intercourse between the sexes than there is between two countries at war. The ladies indeed may ogle and the gentlemen sigh; but an embargo is laid on any closer commerce. At length, to interrupt hostilities, the lady directress or intendant, or what you will, pitches upon a lady and gentleman to walk a minuet, which they perform with a formality that approaches to despondence."

## 27th

**1844:** During the excavations for the Granton Railway, silver and copper coins were found among a pile of human remains all of which were thought to have come from a galleon of the Spanish armada of Philip II. Later diggings revealed even earlier remains and suggested that Granton and Wardie had been occupied by primitive tribes from the neighbouring Wardie Muir. In later years the locality was not without further historical interest: it was there that Sir James Y. Simpson, the pioneer of anaesthesia, lived in a villa in Laverockbank Road and number 70 Trinity Road was once the home of the Ballantyne family, the printers of Sir Walter Scott's novels, and was known, picturesquely, as Harmony Hall. Other notable inhabitants in the nineteenth century were the artist Horatio Macculloch and the poet Alexander Smith.

# September

28th ――――――――――――――――――――――――――――

29th ――――――――――――――――――――――――――――

30th ――――――――――――――――――――――――――――

# September

## 28th

**1660:** William Woodcock inaugurated a hackney coach service between Edinburgh and Leith. The hire of the coach was twelve shillings scots, but if necessary this could be shared amongst four passengers as Woodcock had given notice that he would "wait for another to goes (sic) along with him (the passenger) to pay no more". The coaches followed the line of the earthworks that David Leslie had hurriedly thrown up against the parliamentary army of General Monck, but the experiment was not a success. It was not until 1774 that the decision was taken to widen and pave the earthwork route that eventually became the present-day Leith Walk. With its broad sweep it should be one of the most elegant streets in Edinburgh but it has suffered from bad, disorganised planning and indifferent architecture.

## 29th

**1582:** Having completed his major work, a Latin history of Scotland, the scholar George Buchanan died in his lodgings in Kennedy Close, a pile of substantial, overpopulated masonry which formed part of the crest of the Royal Mile near Hunter Square, and which was within a stone's throw of Walter Scott's birthplace and adjacent to John Dowie's famous tavern. Buchanan was one of the finest European scholars of his day and he had taught in Paris and Portugal before returning to Scotland in 1561 to become tutor to Mary, Queen of Scots. Darnley's murder in 1567 had alienated him from court and he had become one of the leading lights in the Reformation movement, although later historians have tended to castigate him for his relentless persecution of the hapless Queen whom he had once admired.

## 30th

**1513:** The poet Gavin Douglas was made a free burgess of the city of Edinburgh during the troubled days that followed the rout of the Scots army at the Battle of Flodden. Although this was a considerable honour, it was less of a compliment to Douglas and his poetry than a recognition of the power that his family wielded in the city. Douglas was the son of Archibald Douglas, the awesome fifth Earl of Angus, or "Bell the Cat" as he was known after his summary execution at Lauder of James III's low-born favourites. As Bishop of Dunkeld the poet held considerable spiritual and temporal power and unlike most Scottish poets, before or since, Douglas occupied a privileged position in the Scottish political hierarchy. He is best known for his translation into Scots of Vergil's *Aeneid*.

# October

St Giles, High Kirk of Edinburgh, stands four-square to the world in the middle of the Royal Mile and has been a principal place of worship since earliest times. The church is notable for its historic Chapel of the Knights of the Thistle.

# October

1st _____

2nd _____

3rd _____

# October

## 1st

**1788:** On a gallows of his own making Deacon William Brodie was executed following a series of daring crimes within the city. A respectable cabinetmaker and member of the Town Council by day, Brodie was a notorious burglar by night, using his knowledge of locks to break into and rob a succession of premises within the city. After an unsuccessful attempt to rob the General Excise Office in Chessel's Court he was betrayed by an accomplice and although he fled to Holland, he was arrested there and brought back to Edinburgh to face trial before the shocked citizens of the city. The duality of his character, sober citizen by day, outlaw by night, was a source of inspiration for R. L. Stevenson's novel *Jekyll and Hyde*. Brodie lived in Brodie's Close in the Lawnmarket.

## 2nd

**1929:** The Duke and Duchess of York, later to become King George VI and Queen Elizabeth, laid the foundation stone of the Princess Margaret Rose Hospital which was to become one of the leading orthopaedic hospitals in Britain. It admitted its first patients in 1932 and was officially opened a year later. The hospital stands in open ground in the ancient district of Mortonhall and it enjoys an open aspect to the Pentland Hills which lie to the south. Behind the hospital stands the stunted hill of Galachlaw where Cromwell's army camped in 1650 before marching east to defeat the Scottish army at the Battle of Dunbar. There is also some evidence that the hill might have been host to a Roman encampment during the occupation of the Lowlands of Scotland.

## 3rd

**1403:** The first item in the extant printed records of Edinburgh refers to the election of the officers of the merchant guild and it is from this date that the posts of provost (or mayor, although he was never known by that title in Edinburgh), dean of guild and baillie are thought to have their origins. Thus the early regulation of the city was in the hands of the merchants who had formed themselves, like their medieval contemporaries in Europe, into a Guild or Union. The actual title of provost in the document is *Prepositus* and the order of preference within the Town Council for the remaining posts was hotly contested. It was finally fixed in the sixteenth century as Provost, Baillies, Dean of Guild, Treasurer and Counsellors and remained that with some additions until the local government reform of 1975.

# October

4th _____

5th _____

6th _____

# October

4th _____

**1848:** When he arrived in Edinburgh to give a public concert in the Music Hall the Polish composer Frederic Chopin stayed at a house in 10 Warriston Crescent, a quiet curving street beside the Water of Leith. Excitement about his visit had been running high within the city and although he was lionised by Edinburgh society Chopin confessed afterwards that he had been bored by the attentions of the genteel ladies who had insisted on playing the piano in his company, and badly at that. Chopin had been driven from Paris, his second home, during the revolution that led to the Second Empire and his tour of Britain had so weakened him that at his last public performance he had to be carried to the piano. A gift of £1,000 from a generous Scottish friend allowed him to return to Paris where he died in 1849.

5th _____

**1785:** The Italian balloonist Vincenzo Lunardi took off from the grounds of George Heriot's Hospital in a balloon and soared across the Firth of Forth to the village of Ceres in neighbouring Fife. The demonstration fired the city's imagination. Shops were closed, business came to a standstill and a contemporary account reckoned that 80,000 people assembled to watch the departure. Lunardi's one-and-a-half hour flight was not surpassed in Scotland until the following century and he repeated the feat in a flight into East Lothian in December that same year. As a compliment to his achievement Edinburgh ladies took to wearing "Lunardi bonnets" of thin gauze stretched over a wire frame to resemble a balloon. In 1784 James Tytler had risen to 350 feet in a hot-air balloon in the city.

6th _____

**1243:** David de Bernham, the Bishop of St Andrews, visited Edinburgh to consecrate the Church of St Giles. Very little remains of that original Norman church, except perhaps the pillars in the choir, as it was destroyed substantially during the thirteenth and fourteenth-century Wars of Independence against England. In 1385 an English army under King Richard II invaded Scotland and put Edinburgh to the sword and the flame, including the Church of St Giles which was burned to the ground with only its pillars and main gateway left standing. Generous benefactions from the Scottish Royal family enabled the church to be rebuilt and expanded beyond the small Norman church that had been so in keeping with the domestic architecture of the early town.

# October

7th _____

8th _____

9th _____

# October

## 7th

**1552:** The waters of the Nor' Loch which lay in the northern lee of the Castle where now lie the Princes Street Gardens, were the subject of considerable civic concern during the sixteenth century. Much of the outcry was over the dumping of rubbish in the loch and there were a number of proposals to make the waters useful, such as the idea to turn it into an eel farm. The strangest idea was an edict to run the Water of Leith into the loch to increase its volume and therefore to provide the city with an inland harbour. Later in the century an Italian called Marques put up a counter proposal to run a canal from the loch to the sea at Leith and this notion was unsuccessfully revived in the early eighteenth century before the Nor' Loch was finally drained.

## 8th

**1835:** The *Edinburgh Evening Courant* reported that the carriage for the ancient cannon called Mons Meg "gave way with a loud crash to the no small alarm of those who were within hearing". For a year little was done to repair the damage to this historical piece of weaponry that had only been restored to Scotland in 1822 after spending some seventy years in English "captivity" in the Tower of London. The history of Mons Meg is hidden in the mists of antiquity but it is popularly thought to have been cast in Flanders and then brought to Scotland where it has almost become a national mascot. In May 1934 an inferior metal carriage was replaced by an exact replica of the original. Mons Meg is a massive and solid piece of ordinance capable of projecting an iron ball over a mile distance.

## 9th

**1843:** A Music Hall was added to the Assembly Rooms in George Street. Built in 1787 to house the balls or dancing assemblies that were such an integral part of Edinburgh social life, the Assembly Rooms had been extended in 1818 and in 1834. The addition of a Music Hall allowed a greater scope for public concerts, although the music festival which inaugurated the new building made a loss of £600! The novelists Charles Dickens and W. M. Thackeray both gave readings from their work in the Music Hall and the Assembly Rooms provided the setting for Sir Walter Scott's decision to announce himself as the author of the Waverley novels. During the First World War the building was used as a recruiting centre and until recently it was the Festival Club during the Edinburgh Festival.

# October

10th _____

11th _____

12th _____

# October

## 10th

**1922:** King George V and Queen Mary unveiled a statue to King Edward VII in the forecourt of Holyroodhouse which, according to the inscription, "His Scottish subjects have erected this memorial in grateful and loyal remembrance". The King is represented in the robes of the Order of the Knights of the Thistle and it was acknowledged to be a striking likeness. There are three wrought iron gates connected with railings decorated with several armorial bearings and a conventional use of the Thistle and the Rose combined with a stag's head and the Royal coat of arms. The statue was designed by H. S. Gamley, R.S.A., but the forecourt itself was the design of the distinguished architect Washington Browne, R.S.A. Several thousand spectators turned out to view the ceremony.

## 11th

**1776:** An order sent to the firm of potters, William Cadell of Prestonpans, indicates that the firm possessed a pattern book for their wares and also demonstrated to the outside world how important had become their sales overseas. Although the early years of the Cadells were racked by litigation the firm survived to become one of the leading east coast potters producing work of great beauty and originality. Prestonpans and Musselburgh continued to be leading centres of pottery work and in Edinburgh it was concentrated in Portobello where an ample clayfield had supplied William Jameson with the raw materials he needed to produce bricks, tiles and piping for the building trade. Pottery ware followed and with Thomas Rathbone, Portobello remained a major centre until the middle of the nineteenth century.

## 12th

**1554:** After the death of her husband King James V, Mary of Guise had moved, probably to a house on Castlehill because, in her opinion, the Palace of Holyroodhouse was in no fit condition to house the Royal household. Sir William MacDowell, the Master of Works, was paid £1,796 for its restoration and as the bill includes an "item to the laird of Craigmillar for lead and carriage of the same to theik the Great Tower with", it would seem that the roof of the palace had been stripped at some point during the fighting of 1544. Mary moved back into Holyroodhouse at Christmas that year and Mass was said in the Chapel Royal by the canons of Stirling. The Queen-Regent, as she had become, continued to make improvements to the palace until the events of the Reformation struggle forced her to move into the Castle.

# October

13th _____

14th _____

15th _____

# October

## 13th

**1405:** The death occurred of Sir Adam Forrester, the first member of the family of that name to have been connected with the church and lands of Corstorphine, which is today a suburb to the west of Edinburgh on the Glasgow road. For over three hundred years the history of Corstorphine and its church were bound up with the fortunes of the Forresters who were great benefactors to the area. It is not certain how long a church has been on the site but the records show that a building was erected as long ago as 1128. In 1374 the existing chapel was acquired and improved by Sir Adam Forrester, a burgess of Edinburgh who was to become Provost four years later. His close links with the Royal family gave him considerable influence which he was able to use to construct his long disappeared castle on the hill of Corstorphine.

## 14th

**1886:** The Prince of Wales visited the International Exhibition which was being held on the Meadows which lie to the south of the city centre. It had been opened in May and was due to run to the end of November and it was the largest exhibition ever to have been mounted in the city. The central point was a massive hall, including a grand pavilion at the west end of the Meadows which was united to a 970-ft. long range of courts on either side of a central corridor. It was constructed largely of steel and glass and extended to seven acres. A novel feature of the exhibition was that it was provided with electric lighting thus attracting visitors after dark. After the exhibition ended the pavilion was demolished and all that remains of its existence are the stone pillars at the north-west entrance.

## 15th

**1553:** In another vain attempt to clean up the streets of Edinburgh, the Town Council passed an edict that ordered the removal of the piles of household rubbish that had accumulated in the streets. Pigs, too, were banned and lanterns were ordered to be hung up at night to burn from five o'clock until nine o'clock. It had become a common practice to allow farmyard animals to roam the streets at will and those living in the high tenements saw no other way to rid themselves of their household waste than to hurl it down into the streets below. The practice continued until the eighteenth century and it was preceded by a shout of "Gardyloo" which has its origins in the French *"Gardez l'eau"*. To stop the terrible shower the passer-by had to shout in return, "Haud yer hand".

# October

**16th** _____

**17th** _____

**18th** _____

# October

## 16th

**1884:** At a cost of £225,000, the Suburban Railway was opened in Edinburgh and thereby the far-flung suburbs were brought into immediate and speedy contact with the city centre. As a result speculative housing increased, especially to the south of the city in the Blackford Hill area where the substantial rentier houses still stand as monuments to the late Victorian expansion of the city. There was an inner and an outer line to the railway: the inner line ran from Waverley to Haymarket, Gorgie, Morningside, Blackford, Newington, Duddingston, Portobello, and the outer line in the reverse direction back to Waverley. Together with the electric tramcars the railway provided Edinburgh with an unsurpassed public transport system between the two world wars and their substitution by buses was a step backwards.

## 17th

**1951:** In a letter to Bruce Cooper, the student who had proposed him for the Rectorship of the University of Edinburgh, the novelist Evelyn Waugh made the following points about his suitability for the post: "I have never voted in a general election as I have never found a Tory stern enough to command my respect. I should think the best election line would not be my worthiness, but the conspicuous unworthiness of the other candidates. Compton Mackenzie doesn't know me. David Talbot Rice, a professor of yours, is an old friend. He lives at 33 Moray Place. He might help with some personal impressions." The other candidates were Jimmy Logan, Stephen Potter, the Aga Khan and Sir Alexander Fleming who went on to win the election. Waugh was at pains to point out his relationship to Lord Cockburn.

## 18th

**1878:** At his house at 12 James Street in Portobello (now demolished to make way for a red sandstone tenement) the antiquary David Laing died leaving a library of over 12,000 books, many of them precious such as Burns' Kilmarnock edition and a first edition of Spenser's *Faerie Queen*. The library was sold by Sotheby's and raised some £16,000, an unprecedented sum, and there were those in Edinburgh who mourned the breaking up of such a fine private collection. Laing had begun his bibliographical career seventy years earlier when he became a partner in his father's bookselling business on the South Bridge. He was also for many years librarian to the Signet Library. The funeral took place five days later in the New Calton Burying Ground, *The Scotsman* lamenting "the sad blank left in Scottish literary society".

# October

19th _____

20th _____

21st_____

# October

## 19th

**1687:** Alexander Hay, a carpenter and a burgess of the city, gave notice to the Town Council that he had constructed six sedan chairs and that he intended to place them for hire for "ease, benefit and public good". The chairs were to be carried by two men in a smart livery and although there was a standard rate of fares, Hay added a proviso that each passenger would be able to make a bargain. So successful was the experiment that by the eighteenth century sedan chairs were a popular conveyance in Edinburgh and they continued in use until the eighteen-fifties. A notorious incident occurred in 1742 when two drunk sedan chairmen carried a corpse through the streets in their chair. They were punished by imprisonment and their vehicle was burned in public at the city's gallows.

## 20th

**1699:** The first public water supply into the city had been laid as early as 1681 when a German engineer, Peter Bruschi, laid a lead pipe with a three-inch bore from the springs at Comiston into the reservoir at Castle Hill, but the ownership of the lands of Comiston was a matter of conflict between the laird and the Town Council until it was satisfactorily concluded in the latter part of 1699. "The Council subscryved two contracts betwixt them and the Lady Comistoun her sone and his tutors for the sole benefite of all the wells and springs in the lands of Comistoun during her said sones pupillarity for payment of the soume of eighteen pounds." At Comiston Springs Avenue the four original buildings still stand over the springs with their picturesque names, Hare, Fox, Teuchat (Lapwing) and Swan.

## 21st

**1817:** In the first issue of the revamped *Blackwood's Magazine* there appeared the notorious Chaldee Manuscript which satirised the Edinburgh Whigs and their supporters in the mocking language of the Old Testament. Half of the city roared with laughter at its long-forgotten references and the other half bellowed with indignation and ill-concealed rage. The manuscript had been composed by the publisher William Blackwood's henchmen, John Gibson Lockhart, later to be Scott's son-in-law, the poet James Hogg and John Wilson, perhaps better known today as "Christopher North". They caused a literary sensation and as the lawsuits began to pile up against the publisher, further issues of that first edition appeared without the offending pages of the "manuscript".

# October

22nd _____

23rd _____

24th _____

# October

## 22nd

**1557:** John Slowane, a merchant of the city, presented a complaint against William Aikman for maligning him as a "false extentour" who had taxed him above his financial means. The slander does not seem to have been considered a serious offence for the Council's only reaction was to make Aikman confess his fault and to order the two men to become friends again. Taxes, or "extents", as they were called, were a serious business and the inhabitants of the city were liable to pay taxes to the city for the purposes of such things as gifts to the Royal family or entertainments to visitors. After the Reformation, additional money was needed to help the poor and to maintain a City Guard. Taxes were fixed by "extentors", a body comprised of eight merchants and eight craftsmen.

## 23rd

**1861:** On the site of Shakespeare Square which housed the Theatre Royal at the eastern end of Princes Street, Prince Albert, the Prince Consort, laid the foundation stone of the new General Post Office. It was designed by Robert Matheson, architect to the Board of Works for Scotland, and the building's Italianate facade blends in surprisingly well with the cool lines of Robert Adam's Register House which stands on the other side of Princes Street. The Post Office building was opened to the public in 1866 and it cost £120,000 to build, substantially less than its predecessor which was a modest affair in nearby Waterloo Place. The present building houses a philatelic counter and gallery which acts as a public showpiece for the Post Office's Philatelic Bureau.

## 24th

**1369:** The lands of Liberton, which lie to the south of the city and which now form a modern suburb, were granted by King David II to William Ramsay of Dalhousie. Originally the possession of the abbots of Holyrood, the lands of Liberton passed to several owners and the area is bathed in antiquity. A tall peel house, or tower, the property of the barons of Liberton, stood there until 1840 when it was demolished, and the parish church, which was rebuilt in 1815, was supposed to have shared many characteristics with the historic church at Corstorphine. Nether Liberton House, an eighteenth-century coaching inn, is a handsome whitewashed structure with later additions and is still standing, as is the neighbouring Inch House, a seventeenth-century pile which stands in the middle of a public park.

# October

25th _____

26th _____

27th _____

# October

25th _____

**1689:** Oysters were considered to be the staple diet of many
Edinburgh citizens and such was their importance to the economy
that the Council was able to pass an edict fixing their price
at "twelve Shillings Scottis per hundred . . . under the payne of
confiscation of the oysters and a pecuniall fyne". A hundred years
later Robert Fergusson still praised the qualities of this now
expensive delicacy:

> *Whan big as burns the gutters rin,*
> *Gin ye hae catcht a droukit skin,*
> *To Luckie Middlemist's loup in,*
> > *And sit fou snug*
> *O'er oysters and a dram o' gin,*
> > *Or haddock lug.*

26th _____

**1915:** Sydney Goodsir Smith, the poet, was born in New Zealand.

> *And shall she get the richts o' it*
> *A diadem for the brou?*
> *Shall Scotland croun her ain again,*
> *This ancient capital?—*
> *Or sell the thing for scrap?*
> *Or some yankee museum maybe?*
> *I'll be here bidin the answer . . .*
> *Here I be and here I drink,*
> *This is mine, Kynd Kittock's land*
> *For ever and aye while stane shall stand—*
> *For ever and aye till the World's End.*

From his poem *Kynd Kittock's Land*.

27th _____

**1862:** The first printed balance sheet of the fledgling St Cuthbert's
Co-operative Association showed an excess of income over
expenditure of £26.4.0½d. and confirmed to its founders that
they were on a sound financial tack. St Cuthbert's had been founded
in July 1859 by an association of workers from the Edinburgh
and Glasgow Railway at Haymarket and the joiners from a
nearby cabinet works. The first shop was opened four months
later at 50 Fountainbridge at the corner of Ponton Street. Earlier
co-operative movements in the city had failed through a mixture
of inexperience, hostility and lack of support, a fate which almost
overcame St Cuthbert's in its first two years as it struggled to
find a professional staff. St Cuthbert's is still one of the largest
"co-ops" in Britain.

# October

28th _____

29th _____

30th _____

# October

## 28th

**1959:** The Scottish Rugby Union announced the completion of the installation of under-soil heating equipment at the international stadium, Murrayfield. Previously the ground was kept playable during cold spells by the use of straw and tarpaulins but through the S.R.U.'s foresight Murrayfield became the first ever rugby ground to receive an "electric blanket". The first game to have been played there had taken place on 21st March 1925 when the Scottish XV defeated their English opponents by 14 points to 11, thus ending a long sequence of English victories. Sixty thousand spectators—a Scottish record at that time—saw the game and after its expansion in 1935 Murrayfield became the largest rugby stadium in Britain. Today attendances at international matches are limited, after over 90,000 people turned up for the Scotland-Wales game in 1975.

## 29th

**1929:** The dedication service of the Morningside Congregational Church was a reminder to Edinburgh of the relevance of the name "Holy Corner" where Chamberlain Road meets Bruntsfield Place. The new church was built on the site of the old North Morningside Church which had served as a social club for the area between 1863 and 1890. With its elegantly slim tower and pantiled roof the church made a fine contribution to this corner and it is matched only by the perfection of Hippolyte Blanc's Christ Church which stands opposite. Built in 1877 in the French Gothic style this episcopalian church has a steeple of one-hundred-and-forty feet and a hammerbeam roof. The neighbouring Baptist church was rebuilt after a near disastrous fire in 1972.

## 30th

**1878:** The creator of the fantasy *Peter Pan*, James Matthew Barrie, matriculated as a student at the University of Edinburgh. He remained there for four years and supplemented his income by working as a book reviewer for *The Scotsman* and as theatre critic for the *Edinburgh Courant*, experience that was to stand him in good stead when he worked as a freelance writer and journalist in London. While a student Barrie shared lodgings in a top flat in Cumberland Street and the memories of his student days in Edinburgh appeared in his memoir *An Edinburgh Eleven*. Barrie went on to become the most successful dramatist of his generation and a leading figure in the British literary establishment but it is for the "lost boys" of *Peter Pan* that he is best remembered today.

# October

31st_____

**1895:** The Royal Edinburgh Hospital for Sick Children in Sciennes Road was opened by Princess Beatrice. Built at a cost of £47,000 to a design by the architect G. Washington Browne who did so much to adorn the city's south side, the hospital provided beds for one-hundred-and-eighteen children and it was initially thought that these would be used by around seven hundred children a year with over eight thousand being treated in the extensive out-patients' departments. The hospital for treating sick children had its origins in Lauriston Lane near the site of the present Royal Infirmary and it moved for a time to Plewlands House in Morningside before the decision was taken to raise funds for a new purpose-built centre for the medical care of children.

# November

Unliked most major cities, Edinburgh does not sit on a large river. The gentle
Water of Leith, instead, meanders gracefully through the city to meet the major
thoroughfare of the Firth of Forth at the port of Leith. The great estuary gave
Edinburgh access to the ports of northern Europe.

# November

1st _____

2nd _____

3rd _____

# November

## 1st

**1853:** "You are all proud of your city," said the painter and designer John Ruskin at Edinburgh's Philosophical Institution in Queen Street, "surely you must feel it a duty in some sort to justify your pride; that is to say, to give yourselves a *right* to be proud of it. That you were born under the shadow of two fantastic mountains — that you live where from your room windows you can trace the shores of its glittering Firth, are no rightful subjects of pride. You did not raise the mountains, nor shape the shores; and the historical houses of your Canongate, and the broad battlements of your castle, reflect honour upon you only through your ancestors. Before you boast of your city, before you venture to call it yours, ought you not scrupulously to weigh the exact share you have had in adding to it or adorning it . . .?"

## 2nd

**1920:** By Act of Parliament the boundaries of what became known as Greater Edinburgh were marked out and as a result Leith finally became a part of Edinburgh. The relationship between the city and its port had been an uneasy one. Although the Royal Charter of 1329 had made specific mention of Leith, the port area had remained a separate community. Reconstituted as a burgh in 1833, it was only at the turn of the nineteenth century that the remaining open land between Leith and Edinburgh was gradually covered with houses and buildings. The matter was complicated by the sharing of public services such as transport and water and amalgamation of the two burghs became inevitable after the First World War. The Act was fiercely contested by the people of Leith who in a referendum voted six to one against amalgamation.

## 3rd

**1675:** The Town Council agreed that Mr John Young, a student who had studied under the late Professor of Mathematics, James Gregory, should be allowed to teach the subject within the University. Gregory came from Aberdeenshire and before becoming professor at Edinburgh he had worked in St Andrews where most of his important discoveries were made. One of the leading intellectuals of his day, he corresponded with Isaac Newton about the merits of their respective telescopes and during his last years in Edinburgh he was doing pioneering work on astronomy related to the parallaxes of Mercury and Venus and on the distance of the stars to the earth. Gregory's nephews, David and Charles, were also distinguished mathematicians and pioneering humanists.

# November

4th _____

5th _____

6th _____

# November

## 4th

**1903:** To Edinburgh belongs the distinction of housing the first free kindergarten or children's nursery school when Miss Alice Waterston set up an establishment in Galloway's Entry. It continued to function there until 1906 when it moved to Reid's Court and it remained in that building until 1954 when it was taken over by the local education authority and moved across the road to Milton House School. Reminiscing about this pioneering system of education, an anonymous contributor to *The Scotsman* wrote in February 1913: "Instead of weakening the responsibility of the parents, the experience has been that it has strengthened it. The parents fully realise the invaluable help the kindergarten has been, and the splendid work it is doing. . . ."

## 5th

**1689:** Guy Fawkes' night was first proclaimed as a public celebration in Edinburgh during the reign of William and Mary by the following edict from the Town Council: ". . . a solemnitie upon the fyfth of November by putting forth of bonfires or the ringing of bells and shooting of cannons from the Castle In testimonie of their great joy for his Majesties birthday . . . And his being instrumental under god for freeing the Kingdomes from poperie and arbitrarie power And for the happy preservation of the kings majesties Ancestors and nobilitie from that horrid plott of the gun powder treason designed to have been execute upon the said fyfth of November during the reigne of their Majesties great Grandfathers King James the sixth." It has remained a popular celebration ever since.

## 6th

**1667:** "Haveing considered the complaint givin in be severall nighbours in and about Fishmercat Close The Councell discharges all persons whatsoever to sell or vent at the said mercat close any maner of fishes als weell dry fish as uther fishes and herring bot to repair to the ordinair mercat places thereof under such paines and penalties as the Magistrats sall inflict and farder the Councell ordains that the bailyies of the quarter every yeir sie this act punctuallie and exactly observed and keeped." Despite the Council's threats, Fishmarket Close continued to be used for the purpose of selling fish and later the "stinking ravine" as it was known came to be a poultry market. The close housed the dwelling of the city hangman and George Heriot lived there for a time.

# November

7th _____

8th _____

9th _____

# November

## 7th

**1802:** Somewhat to their astonishment the editors of the newly founded *Edinburgh Review* discovered that they had to put in hand a further printing of 750 copies of that issue and had become one of the best-selling magazines of its day. The new journal was the brainchild of an Anglican chaplain, Sydney Smith, who had said that "it requires a surgical operation to get a joke well into a Scotch understanding", and three advocates — Henry Brougham, Francis Horner and Francis Jeffrey, who was to become the sole editor. He vested the role editor with a previously unheard of dignity and was paid a substantial salary by the publisher Archibald Constable who also arranged that contributors should be paid, another welcome innovation.

## 8th

**1847:** Chloroform was first used in an obstetrical case by Sir James Young Simpson in a house at 19 Albany Street. The patient was Jane Carstairs, a doctor's wife who had recently returned from India to live in Fife, but who had decided to spend her confinement in Edinburgh as her first baby had been still-born in a terrible, painful birth. Simpson had been experimenting first with ether and then with chloroform, as it seemed to possess all the benefits of a good anaesthetic: "By moistening, with $\frac{1}{2}$ a teaspoonful of the liquid, a pocket handkerchief rolled into a funnel shape . . ." Jane Carstairs gave birth, successfully and painlessly, to a daughter Wilhelmina who kept in touch with Simpson for the rest of her life. The new drug was used in surgery at the Royal Infirmary two days later.

## 9th

**1904:** On the site of the Morningside smiddy which was owned by J. & W. Denholm, a firm which had its beginnings in the early years of the century, a new public library was opened. Denholms' smiddy and its adjoining cottage had been demolished in the previous year, bringing to an end a picturesque period in the history of the village of Morningside. At the end of the nineteenth century there were two other blacksmiths in addition to Denholm in Morningside, one being Dick Wright, whose smiddy was a centre of gossip and well remembered for its roaring bellows and the fiery forge. The new library was opened by the Lord Provost's son John Harrison, who was later to become the City Treasurer, and its initial stock was 6,000 books.

# November

10th _____

11th _____

12th _____

# November

## 10th

**1646:** A charter was granted by the Crown in favour of James, Duke of Hamilton, appointing him and his heirs male Heritable Keepers of Holyroodhouse. By virtue of this charter the Hamiltons became the guardians of the palace and bailies of the Abbey Sanctuary. This latter curiosity provided a residence for aristocratic debtors, and still stands among the sixteenth-century buildings on the left-hand side of the Abbey Strand outside the gates of Holyroodhouse. Within the confines of the sanctuary, which included Holyrood Park and Arthur's Seat, the "Abbey Lairds", as they were known, could live in complete freedom from the claims of their debtors. On Sundays they were free to venture back into the city but the custom ended when imprisonment for debt was abolished in 1880.

## 11th

**1675:** The Town Council ordered the Riding of the Marches, a ceremony that over the centuries had taken place on a Hallowe'en, to coincide with All Hallows Fair. Preceded by the Provost, the Town Council, armed and on horseback, would parade slowly round the boundaries of Edinburgh and in the evening they would be entertained to a splendid supper. Gradually the ceremony fell into disuse and by 1718, the last recorded date of its occurrence, it had become little more than a picturesque memory of the past. It was only in 1946 that it was revived to celebrate the end of the war. On that occasion the cavalcade marched only from Holyroodhouse to the Mercat Cross, as a complete circuit of the modern city would have been an impossible task for the mounted horsemen.

## 12th

**1772:** In Ruddiman's *Weekly Magazine or Edinburgh Amusement*, the poet Robert Fergusson published "Hallow Fair", his vividly comic description of the annual fair held in the first week of November at Castle Barns, near the modern Fountainbridge:

> *At Hallowmas, whan nights grow lang,*
> *And starnies shine fu' clear,*
> *Whan fock, their nippin cald to bang,*
> *Their winter hap-warms wear,*
> *Near Edinburgh a fair there hads,*
> *I wat there's nane whase name is,*
> *For strappin dames and sturdy lads,*
> *And cap and stoup, mair famous*
> *Than it that day.*

# November

13th _____

14th _____

15th _____

# November

## 13th

**1093:** Malcolm III, or "Canmore" (the great head or chief) as he was known, was killed at the Battle of Alnwick while leading his army against King Rufus of England. Malcolm was one of the first Scottish kings to use Edinburgh as a base and he had built a hunting lodge on the Castle rock for his expeditions into the Drumsheugh Forest which lay to the south. For his wife St Margaret he built a chapel — it now stands within the safety of the Castle's walls — which is generally held to be the oldest building in the city. The Queen died three days after her husband in Dunfermline, having had to escape from the hunting lodge. According to the the historian John of Fordun it was a miraculous occurrence: "Some indeed tell us that during the whole of that journey a cloudy mist was round that family. . . ."

## 14th

**1694:** Twelve soldiers of the City Guard convoyed a number of women prisoners to Glasgow following the petition of "James Montgomerie younger merchant in Glasgow shewing that being informed that ther is in ther Correction house severall dissoluit women whom the Councill were desirous to have transported to America and he having at present occasion to send from Glasgow a vessell thither Therfore he offered to receave what number of such dissoluit people can be got betuixt twenty and thretty two he being payed thretty shilling starling for each to be imployed in cloathing and other necessars for ther transportation and lykeways being allowed a compitent number of souldiers for guarding them to the toune of Glasgow . . . that they shall be transported to America . . .".

## 15th

**1824:** The most disastrous fire recorded in the city broke out on a Monday night in a seven-storey tenement at the head of Assembly Close. All the buildings on the south side of the High Street down to Parliament Square were destroyed in the flames, together with the buildings that ran down to the Cowgate. The dry wooden panelling and close proximity of the houses produced a fierce blaze that was impossible to control and at the height of the fire burning cinders fell on neighbouring houses, adding to the conflagration. On the following day the steeple of the Tron Kirk caught fire and molten lead cascaded onto the street below before the whole edifice collapsed. Twenty-four fire engines fought the fire that made 400 families homeless and caused £200,000 worth of damage.

*Edinburgh from Braid Hills*

# November

16th _____

17th _____

18th _____

# November

## 16th

**1956:** The date for the running of the last city tram had been
fixed earlier in the year and throughout the week enthusiasts
had photographed and recorded those transports of delight
that shuddered noisily but efficiently through the city's streets.
The last remaining services, 23 and 28, completed their journeys
and returned to the Shrubhill depot and at 6.57 p.m., the last
scheduled service run by car 88 left Stanley Road en route
for Tollcross before returning to the Leith Walk depot.
Then a convoy of trams, led by a decorated car with car 217
in the rear made its stately way through the thronged streets.
The current for the tramway system was finally switched
off at 9.40 p.m. bringing to an end half a century of Edinburgh
trams.

## 17th

**1587:** In the wake of the reformation of the church in Scotland,
the Town Council of Edinburgh passed a number of edicts
against the vice, drunkenness and prostitution it associated with
the pageants and festivals that formed the principal entertainments
within the city. Through the Council's zeal a law was passed
to expel from Edinburgh "all menstralis, pyperis, fidleris,
common sangsteris, and specially of badrie and filthy sangs, and
siclyke all vagabounds and maisterless persouns quha hes na
seruice nor honest industrie to leif be". Although it was impossible
to ban every kind of public entertainment, the city's fathers have
continued to keep a beady eye on the theatre and even up to
the present day, dramatic entertainments have been subject to
occasional civic disapproval.

## 18th

**1668:** Before the foundation of the Royal College of Physicians in
1681 quacks and mountebanks frequently interfered with the
proper practice of medicine. Sometimes they indulged in other
illegal pranks as this extract from the Records of the Old Tolbooth
illustrates: "Sir bailie, Thes are only to transmitt to your prisone
oure being unsufficient the persone of James Vallentyn, a man who
takevpon him to practice divinaone & soothsaying and ffor money
doeth ordenarly make a trade of discovering things lost & qr they
may be found, And by qm they war taiken away or stollen . . . Wee
belive him to be a louse fflagitious ffellow and therfor Recommend
him to be strickly keepe in prisson till he be presented by on
james Dun serjant to the garison of the castell of Edr . . . yor very
humbill servants the byillies of Leith."

# November

19th ——————————————————————————

20th ——————————————————————————

21st——————————————————————————

# November

## 19th

**1776:** Papermaking was an early and profitable industry in Edinburgh, with waterpowered mills at Dalry, Spylaw, Colinton and Cramond. There were also several important mills outside the city principally in the village of Penicuik which remained a centre for many years. One of the earliest mills was owned by the Watkins family and an advertisement in the *Edinburgh Advertiser* announced its sale after some fifty years of business. "Papermill to let . . . the Papermill at Pennycuik etc. with the whole machinery houses and others pertaining thereto lately belonging to Mr Watkins . . . There are 2 vats in the mill which is plentifully supplied with the very finest spring water conducted in lead pipes." Watkins was printer to the Royal Bank of Scotland and introduced the use of watermarks on bank notes.

## 20th

**1697:** The original statutes of the Merchant Maiden Hospital were framed along the lines of its benefactor's instructions to the Merchant Company of 14th June 1694. "Mary Erskine, relict of James Hair, druggist, had mortified 10,000 merks for the maintenance of burges children of the female sex and that the money was actually left to the town of Edinburgh for that effect." Very little is known about the facts of Mary Erskine's life and only her name survives as a testament to her generosity. She also gave money to the Trades Maiden Hospital which grew into something of a rival to its older sister institution. The Merchant Maiden Hospital opened in the Cowgate and has had subsequent premises in Bristo and Lauriston. The hospital is now known as the Mary Erskine School, the oldest of the Merchant Company schools.

## 21st

**1678:** "The councill elects Captain Craufoord ane of the merchant councillors to be Captain of the orange company and moderator of the Captains. . . ." Behind that seemingly routine statement in the records of the Town Council lies a wealth of little known traditions related to the well being of the early city. In 1580 the Trained Bands of Edinburgh — or Town Companies as they were also known — were constituted to take the place of the old levy of burgesses for service in the King's army. Captains of the Guards were selected by the Town Council and the sixteen companies had different colours or combinations of colours. A Society of Captains was formed in 1663 with the Captain of the Orange Colours as leader, a post that soon became a ceremonial one within the city.

# November

22nd _____

23rd _____

24th _____

# November

## 22nd

**1888:** The Corporation of the City of Edinburgh agreed to purchase the Braid Hills which lie to the south of the city beyond Blackford Hill. Two years previously the Town Council had banned the game of golf from Bruntsfield Links and those golfers who did not belong to any of the city's leading golf clubs began a campaign for a new civic golf course. The land on the Braid Hills was suggested, but many councillors felt that it was too far removed from the city centre and the battle dragged on until 1888 when a party of councillors, using the newly constructed suburban railway, walked to the Braid Hills and decided to proceed with a scheme that had been mooted by the *Evening Dispatch*. The Braids now boast two courses which were ready for play in September 1889.

## 23rd

**1814:** On a dark winter evening David Loch, a carter from Biggar, was pulled from his horse as he was crossing the Braid burn near the present-day entrance to the Hermitage of Braid. He was then knocked on the head and robbed of most of his possessions. During the attack his cries for help were answered by a farrier at the nearby Braidburn Farm who carried Loch to the house of a Mr Scott in Myreside. Two men were arrested for the robbery — Thomas Kelly and Henry O'Neil and they were tried before the Lord Justice Clerk for highway robbery and sentenced to death. It was stipulated by the judge that sentence should be carried out at the scene of the crime and in January 1815 the two men were led out to the Braid burn bridge to be hanged, the last men to be executed for highway robbery in Scotland.

## 24th

**1861:** At one o'clock on a quiet Sunday morning at the beginning of winter the tenement house which stood between 99 and 103 High Street crashed to the ground taking with it seven storeys, their inhabitants and fifty-five lives. Rescue workers and the fire brigade worked throughout the night to find survivors and towards dawn they had all but given up hope of further life existing in the dust and rubble. Then from within the debris a boy's voice called out: "Heave awa' chaps, I'm no dead yet!" He was pulled out virtually unharmed and the remarkable incident is commemorated in a stone carving of a boy's head above the present-day Paisley Close and the house now standing there has come to be known as "Heave Awa Hoose".

# November

25th _____

26th _____

27th _____

# November

## 25th

**1681:** General Tam Dalyell of the Binns was appointed Colonel of a new regiment of horse which was to be styled the Royal Regiment of Scots Dragoons, or, as it was to be better known, the Royal Scots Greys. Dalyell refused to adopt the scarlet coats commonly worn by regiments of the British army and clothed his men in grey, thus giving one derivation for the regiment's name; the other is from the grey horses which the third colonel, Sir Thomas Livingstone, introduced at the turn of the seventeenth century. The Greys took part in the Covenanting wars and gained for themselves a reputation as a stern, uncompromising police force. By the seventeen hundreds and thereafter they were in action in the European wars in the accustomed role of heavy cavalry. The regimental museum is in Edinburgh Castle.

## 26th

**1661:** After the Restoration, the Palace of Holyroodhouse became once more the centre of Scottish affairs and was used as the meeting place for the Scottish Privy Council under the powerful Secretary of State the Earl of Lauderdale. During Cromwell's occupation the palace had been repaired, but a minute of the Privy Council was still able to complain of "the defective parts of the Palace of Holyrude-house so much thereof as is presently habitable and under roof". This complaint may have had something to do with Lauderdale's own love of building — he had built Thirlestane for himself in the Borders and had improved his town house of Bruntsfield — though there is little doubt that the palace was in any case in need of attention. The task was given to Sir William Bruce who gave the palace the shape we know today.

## 27th

**1680:** The last prisoners taken from the defeated Covenanting army after the Battle of Bothwell Bridge were transported overseas from Edinburgh. They had been held in conditions of utmost deprivation in the long cemetery in the south-west corner (Greyfriars churchyard), and many of the leaders had been hanged, often in a mood of religious exaltation, at mass executions in the Grassmarket. One of the ships transporting the Covenanters to the Barbados was lost off the Orkneys and all aboard were drowned. The Covenanters, who looked on compromise with the government on the question of religion as a betrayal of the National Covenant of 1638, were put down with considerable ferocity by the Lord Advocate, Sir George Mackenzie of Rosehaugh, and by Graham of Claverhouse, "Bonny Dundee".

# November

28th _____

29th _____

30th _____

# November

## 28th

**1786:** Riding high on the success of the publication in July that
year of his *Poems, Chiefly in the Scottish Dialect*, Robert Burns
arrived in Edinburgh to further his career as a poet. He lodged
with a Mrs Carfrae in Baxter's Close in the Lawnmarket, and he
was quickly taken up by the *literati* who were anxious to pay
homage to this "heaven-taught ploughman". Writing to his
close friend, the Ayrshire lawyer Gavin Hamilton, Burns admitted,
somewhat self-deprecatingly, that he was in danger of becoming
"the eighth Wise Man of the world", but his visit to Edinburgh
brought about the publication of a second collection of poems,
paid for by the gentlemen of the Caledonian Hunt under the
patronage of the Earl of Glencairn. Burns returned to the city
in December 1787.

## 29th

**1792:** At his house of New Hailes which lay between Musselburgh
and Niddrie House, the home of the Wauchope family, died
the distinguished judge and man of letters, Sir David Dalrymple,
Lord Hailes. The house had long been famed for the library which
Lord Hailes had built up, and although he gained a certain amount
of notoriety for being one of the presiding judges at the trial of
Deacon Brodie, it is as an historian and man of letters that
Hailes is best remembered. During his lifetime he added immensely
to Scottish antiquarian scholarship and was responsible for
editing the Bannatyne Manuscript which contained the work
of Dunbar, Douglas, Lindsay, Scott and other sixteenth century
poets which might otherwise have been lost to posterity. He also
wrote *Annals of Scotland*.

## 30th

**1962:** On each St Andrew's Day, it was once the habit of the B.B.C.
in Scotland to invite a distinguished Scot to give a radio lecture
on the state of the nation. The 1962 lecture — "A Mind for the
Future" — was given in Edinburgh by John Grierson, one of the
founding fathers of the documentary film movement. He began
be declaring his intentions: "The declaration of one's loyalties is
always a very proper and agreeable duty" and went on to speak
warmly about his childhood days in Stirling and Glasgow. He kept
his sharp words for the mass media: "I don't think it is a living
culture we are seeing reflected: a living culture out and about, like
old Adam Smith in his day, in the living present, forging a mind
for our tomorrows: rather a culture, all too often, of the cultural
conceits and the culturally conceited."

# December

Princes Street, Edinburgh's fairest, though most altered street, contains the city's principal shops and it also offers the finest view of the Castle and of the long sweep of the old town. As no building is permitted on that south side the historic view is protected for future generations.

# December

1st _____

2nd _____

3rd _____

# December

## 1st

**1681:** The first recorded meeting of the Company of the Merchants of Edinburgh took place in the High Council House under the presidency of the Lord Provost, Sir James Fleming. Its business was to elect the office-bearers that had been set down in the Royal Charter granted to the Company in October that same year. The Company's original aims were to provide a forum for Edinburgh's merchants and traders, to establish a code of conduct and to set up an insurance fund for widows and orphans. As such it owed its origins to the earlier medieval merchant guilds who provided the members of the first town councils. By the nineteenth century it had assumed control of some of the leading private schools in the city, and the Merchant Company still plays an important role in the city's politics.

## 2nd

**1668:** By edict the Town Council ordained that "the haill candlemakers of this burgh to keip mercat dayes each weik Tuesday Wednesday and Fryday and the mercat place to be betwixt Neddries Wynd head and Blackfrier Wynd head for selling their candle and that they sell non under ane pund weight and the mercat tyme to be betwixt nyne houris in the foirnoon and tuo hours in the afternoone and that no person cry any candle through the streit bot that they be sold in the publict mercat or in ther chops". The candlemakers were only one of a number of guilds within the city which had been founded to protect the needs of their members and to negotiate rights with the Town Council. Remains of their importance can be seen in the names of some of the wynds in the Royal Mile.

## 3rd

**1897:** The University's new graduation hall, the McEwan Hall, was officially opened by a future Prime Minister, A. J. Balfour, on whom the honorary degree of LL.D. was conferred at the subsequent graduation ceremony. The hall cost £110,000 to build and most of the cost was defrayed by Sir William McEwan, M.P. for Central Edinburgh and a member of the famous Edinburgh brewing family. With a capacity for 2,200 people the hall is in the form of a Greek theatre and has the distinguishing feature of two adjoining external stair towers each of which has a double spiral staircase. There is also a fine organ with 3,000 stops and is further distinguished by being the first building in Britain to use steel tresses in its domed roof. Today it stands as the centre point of the University's redevelopment.

# December

4th _____

5th _____

6th _____

# December

4th _____

**1894:** One of Edinburgh's best known, and certainly best loved writers, the novelist and poet Robert Louis Stevenson, died at his adopted home in Samoa in the South Pacific. Even at the end of his life Edinburgh was pulling at his heart-strings for in the manuscript of his last novel, *Weir of Hermitage*, his wife Fanny found the dedicatory verse to her which is also a hymn of praise to the "precipitous city" he had left for ever six years before:

> *I saw rain falling and the rainbow drawn*
> *On Lammermuir. Hearkening I heard again*
> *In my precipitous city beaten bells*
> *Winnow the keen sea wind. And here afar*
> *Intent on my own place and race I wrote.*

5th _____

**1905:** Following a visit to Edinburgh the novelist G. K. Chesterton wrote his impressions of the city in the *Daily News:* "The beauty of Edinburgh as a city is absolutely individual, and consists in one separate atmosphere and one separate class of qualities. It consists chiefly in a quality that may be called 'abruptness', an unexpected alternation of heights and depths. It seems like a city built on precipices: a perilous city. Although the actual ridges and valleys are not (of course) really very high or very deep, they stand up like strong cliffs; they fall like open chasms. There are turns of the steep street that take the breath away like a literal abyss. There are thoroughfares, full, busy, and lined with shops, which yet give the emotions of an Alpine stair. It is, in the only adequate word for it, a sudden city."

6th _____

**1866:** The Chalmers Memorial Free Church, one of the first churches of that denomination to be built in the city, was opened in the Grange at the corner of Chalmers Crescent and Grange Road. It took its name from the first Moderator of the Free Church of Scotland, Dr Thomas Chalmers, who lies buried in the neighbouring Grange cemetery. Chalmers had been one of the leaders of the Disruption of May 1843 when the established church had come into conflict with those members who disagreed with the methods of selecting ministers for parishes in Scotland. He was also a powerful evangelist who did much to help the poor and to focus society's attention on the problems caused by poverty. The church is now known as the parish church of St Catherine's in Grange.

# December

7th _____

8th _____

9th _____

# December

## 7th

**1889:** The Edinburgh Skating Club held its traditional annual dinner and as usual the toast of "Jack Frost" took precedence over the loyal toast. The club had its beginnings in the eighteenth century when Duddingston Loch and Lochend began to be used for organised skating and the motto "Ocurior Euro" — "swifter than the east wind" — was chosen by the first members. Several distinguished Edinburgh men joined the club, including Lord Cockburn, William Adam and the Tytlers of Woodhouselee, and skating enjoyed a vogue as a social sport for many years. A distinguishing feature of the club was its penchant for devising elaborate movements, and the records show that amongst others, the following figures had to be perfected by the club: The Worm or Screw, Crossing, The Wild Goose.

## 8th

**1727:** The Royal Bank of Scotland opened for business at its office in Ship Close, now known as Old Stamp Office Close, off the Royal Mile. It had its origins in the "equivalents" — a system of payments made by the government to Scotland after the Act of Union in compensation for the Darien Scheme — and in the end of the twenty-one-year-old monopoly of the Bank of Scotland. The Royal Bank issued its own notes, a practice it continues to this day, and it was the first British bank to introduce the concept of "cash credit" or overdraft. In 1969 the bank merged with the National Commercial Bank of Scotland, and its head office is on the east side of St Andrew Square next to Dundas House, a branch office and former town house of Sir Laurence Dundas.

## 9th

**1767:** The Canongate Theatre, the first house in the city in which dramatic events were performed under official licence, opened with a performance of *The Earl of Essex* with a specially written prologue composed by James Boswell. Earlier it had been the scene of a riot between a group of young advocates and a party of students which had so fallen out of hand that the City Guard had been called to restore order. However, the Guards were terrified of entering a house of disrepute (as the theatre was commonly held to be in Edinburgh) and their captain had to take the lead by leaping on to the stage with an encouraging shout. The ruse would have worked had not one of the students pulled the trapdoor on which the bold captain stood, and he disappeared from view to the consternation of the retreating Guards.

# December

10th _____

11th _____

12th _____

# December

## 10th

**1688:** At the time of the Glorious Revolution when James II fled
the country and William and Mary of Orange were proclaimed
monarchs of Britain in his place, Edinburgh was in a great state of
excitement. A mob attacked Holyroodhouse and broke into
the Chapel Royal intent on destroying all manifestations of
popery. The woodwork was ripped out and hauled up to the
Mercat Cross where it was ceremonially burned, and in a
frenzy the Royal burial vaults were opened and the bones
thrown out. The Chancellor, the Earl of Perth, was forced to flee
from the city and for a few weeks anarchy prevailed on the city's
streets. A rumour that a large Irish army was about to invade
Scotland to support James renewed anti-Catholic feelings, and a mob
of students burned an effigy of the Pope in the High Street.

## 11th

**1687:** One of the most curious diaries of life in Edinburgh
was that of Thomas Kincaid, a surgeon-apothecary who lived
and worked in the city. Unlike other contemporary documents
which merely record events, Kincaid took the trouble to
express his own thoughts in a vivid and amusing style — "I
thought upon" is a common beginning to his almost daily
entries. He was also capable of a certain wryness, often making
little of dreadful events such as the anti-Popish riot on the
previous day when "Captain Wallace caused his men fire
twise a running fire amongst them, whereby five or six of them
were killed and many of them deadly wounded". His entry is
simply: "I went down to the Abay and saw them searching for
Wallace. They got some of his men but not himselfe."

## 12th

**1913:** A representative company of church leaders and social
temperance reformers met in Darling's Regent Hotel in Waterloo
Place to celebrate the golden jubilee of one of Edinburgh's
oldest temperance hotels — the oldest in the city being the Old
Waverley in Princes Street, founded in 1848. During the speeches
which followed a "sumptuous dinner", special mention was
made of the fact that one of the hotel's main attractions — other
than the absence of alcohol — were the prayer meetings for guests
held in the drawing-room each evening. The hotel remained in
family hands until 1963 when it was bought by the North British
Trust Hotels Group who, with no regard for history, licensed the
hotel and named their cocktail bar Darling's. Fate had its revenge
though, as the hotel closed its doors forever in 1976.

# December

13th ─────────────────────────────

14th ─────────────────────────────

15th ─────────────────────────────

# December

## 13th

**1734:** Panmure Close in the Canongate once gave access to Panmure House, the town house of the Earl of Panmure who lived there during the early part of the eighteenth century. Its most famous resident was the economist Adam Smith, the author of *The Wealth of Nations* who died there in 1790. After lying empty for many years, this fine rubble-built mansion with its distinctive crow-stepped gables was restored by Lord Thomson of Fleet, the owner of *The Scotsman*, who gave it to the Canongate Boys' Club. Since 1973 it has been used as a young people's training centre, entered now from the neighbouring Little Lochend Close. The close was once known as Bassendyne's Close because Alison, the daughter of the printer Thomas Bassendyne, once lived there. There is a mention of it in the protocol book of George Irving.

## 14th

**1756:** At his theatre in the Canongate, the actor-manager West Digges produced "A *New Tragedy* called DOUGLAS, by an ingenious gentleman of this country". The play's author was in fact an East Lothian minister called John Home and its production caused a sensation within the city. On the first night the packed audience was divided between those who were on hand to applaud the new national drama and those of more spiritual disposition who had come to deplore the ungodly spectacle of a minister of the church abetting the seat of Satan, the theatre. Home was subsequently persecuted by the church and forced to resign his post, but the first night of his *Douglas* has become famous for the oft-quoted remark of an enthusiastic member of the audience who shouted out, "Where's your Wullie Shakespeare noo?".

## 15th

**1865:** In his book *Edinburgh: Picturesque Notes* R. L. Stevenson wrote that the Hunter's Tryst in the area of Oxgangs was haunted by a spirit much given to loud moans. That he had not troubled to check his facts is suggested more prosaically by an article in *The Echo*, written some dozen or so years before Stevenson put pen to paper: "The ghost took the form of a long moan, especially noisy when there was a west wind present. Rather undramatically the ghost was laid by the discovery that it was loudest at the line of pipes that conveyed the water from Bonaly reservoir to Edinburgh. The pipes ran from Bonaly close by the entrance to Howden Glen linking up with the Swanston water supply, and then past Hunter's Tryst to the city. The ghost was noisiest after dry weather. . . ."

# December

16th _____

17th _____

18th _____

# December

## 16th

**1810:** Jenny Allan, the daughter of Robert Allan, a banker and the owner of the newspaper the *Caledonian Mercury*, kept one of the most intimately private diaries of her generation in Edinburgh. Something of her style can be seen in this typical entry. "After tea popped over to the Theatre where I had difficulty in getting a seat in the low boxes. The opera of The Siege of Belgrade & Braham were the attractions — having heard him often before I confess I felt little, he never was a singer to my taste, he over enriches & eternally ornamenting & altho' he can scarcely spoil, Nature having given him so exquisite a voice, yet he runs lamentably wide of good taste. His ornaments remind me of a coarse yet striking Irish allusion, 'like spreading butter upon fat'." Jenny married John Harden and lived at 29 Queen Street.

## 17th

**1600:** In the quiet suburb of Stockbridge which lay within the jurisdiction of the Baron Bailies of Broughton, there took place one of the most infamous abductions in Edinburgh's history. A group of horsemen led by John Kincaid of Craighouse broke down the doors of the house of Bailie John Johnstone and abducted Isobel Hutcheon, a widow dwelling in "sober, quiet and peaceable manner for the time, dreading naw evil, harm, pursuit or injury of any persons". Kincaid was accused later that he "pat violent hands on the said Isobel's person, took her captive, reft, ravished and took her away with him to his place of Craighouse". It was only the threat of force from King James VI and the Earl of Mar that made Kincaid surrender his captive, though his punishment was laughable — a small fine and the surrender of his horse.

## 18th

**1825:** The printer James Ballantyne called at the home of Sir Walter Scott at 39 North Castle Street to announce the impending bankruptcy of their company and the ruin that stared them all in the face. Scott's Journal for the day is a mixture of stoicism and sadness as he faced up to an uncertain future. "What a life mine has been. Half educated, almost wholly neglected or left to myself — stuffing my head with most nonsensical trash and undervalued in society for a time by most of my companions — getting forward and held a bold and clever fellow contrary to the opinion of all who thought me a mere dreamer. . . . Rich & poor four or five times — once on the verge of ruin yet opend new souces of wealth almost overflowing. . . . And what is the end of it? God knows & so ends the catechism."

# December

19th _____

20th _____

21st _____

# December

## 19th

**1739:** The committee of the Dean Orphanage Hospital, one of the city's oldest charities, appointed a "Master to cause the boys heads be combed duly every day and particularly every Saturday night the childrens heads be combed and powdered with flour as also that the master order the childrens feet be washed at least each fourteen days upon Saturday". The orphanage had been established in 1733 under the auspices of the Society for Propagating Christian Knowledge and the first building was in Bailie Fyfe's Close. This was too cramped for efficient operation and a building was designed for the orphanage by William Adam, in the grounds of Trinity Hospital. By the beginning of the nineteenth century they had moved again to Dean House. The last Dean Orphanage is now Lothian Region's Dean Education Centre.

## 20th

**1681:** One of the many daring escapes in the annals of Edinburgh took place at the Tolbooth when the Earl of Argyle, under a sentence of death that was to be carried out the followng day, walked out to freedom in the disguise of the servant to his daughter-in-law Lady Sophia Lindsay of Balcarres. Argyle had been imprisoned for refusing to sign the Test Act and his opportunity to escape came when Lady Sophia disguised him as her footman during her last visit to him. The plan nearly came to grief when a soldier grasped Argyle's arm roughly and he was on the point of retaliation when Lady Sophia slapped his face and exclaimed, to the soldier's delight, "Thou careless loon!". Lady Sophia was imprisoned briefly for her part in the escape and Argyle was recaptured in 1685.

## 21st

**1903:** The Caledonian Hotel was opened as part of the terminus of the headquarters of the Caledonian Railway Company. It started life as the Princes Street Station Hotel and although it came to be called the Caledonian it has always been known locally as the "Caley". Built in red sandstone, the interior rings to the luxurious elegance of bygone days and its telegraphic address, "Luxury, Edinburgh", was no exaggeration. Over the years it maintained standards of top service and catering and between 1928 and 1938 its Pompadour Restaurant offered the finest French cuisine in the city. Until recently the Caley belonged to the British Transport Hotels group along with its sister railway hotel at the other end of Princes Street, the North British Hotel.

# December

22nd _____

23rd _____

24th _____

# December

## 22nd

**1917:** Wilfred Owen, one of the major poets of the First World War, left Edinburgh for the last time, being killed on the western front in August the following year. He had been a patient at Craiglockhart Hospital and it was there that he had met his fellow poet and soldier Siegfried Sassoon who was being treated for a "nervous breakdown" following his refusal to continue fighting in the war. The two men became close friends and collaborators during their time in Edinburgh and it was in the former hydropathic hotel that Owen had written his major statements "Anthem for Doomed Youth" and "Dulce et decorum est". For a period Owen taught English at Tynecastle secondary school and he enjoyed taking the pupils on long walks into the Pentland Hills.

## 23rd

**1932:** The Dean of Guild Court made an order for the partial demolition of Advocates' Close which was once considered to be one of the most fashionable parts of the High Street. The close had been visited by members of this committee whose task it was to monitor building regulations in the city, and as it had been found to be in "a ruinous and unsure and dangerous state", it was decided to proceed immediately with the demolition. Tenants in the affected houses had to be removed while work was in progress but great pains were taken to ensure the retention of the architectural and historical associations of the close and its surroundings. In 1956 the buildings at the head of the close were again found to be in an advanced state of decay and had to be rebuilt completely.

## 24th

**1856:** In his house at Shrub Hill, Portobello, the remarkable self-taught geologist Hugh Miller killed himself by firing a bullet into his left lung. His body was found the following day together with a suicide note to his wife: "My brain burns, I must have walked; and a fearful dream lies upon me". A verdict was passed of suicide "Under the impulse of sanity", and by a tragic mischance, the gunsmith called in to unload Miller's revolver was killed when it was accidentally discharged. Miller was one of the leading scientists of his day, and as a committed adherent to the Free Church he may have found it difficult to reconcile his church's strict belief in the Creation with his geological findings. His best known books are *The Old Red Sandstone* and *My Schools and Schoolmasters*.

# December

25th _____

26th _____

27th _____

# December

### 25th

**1841:** To celebrate Christmas Day, Charles Drummond, a Leith printer and publisher, produced what is thought to have been the first ever Yuletide card in Britain, and sold it from his shop in the Kirkgate. The idea had been given to him by his friend Thomas Strurrock of Trinity and the card showed a smiling, chubby-cheeked boy with the legend: "A Gude New Year,/And mony o' them". The idea was taken up elsewhere and the first distinctive Christmas card was produced in London two years later. With the Victorian emphasis on Christmas as one of the great annual festivals, and on Santa Claus and Christmas trees, Christmas gradually began to enjoy a revival of popularity in Edinburgh after its relative obscurity in the years following the Reformation in the sixteenth century.

### 26th

**1834:** On St Stephen's Day, or Boxing Day as it came to be known in the secular Victorian calendar, the convent of St Margaret in Whitehouse Loan was opened by two Scottish sisters of the order of Ursulines. It was the first convent in post-Reformation Scotland and there were those who thought that it was premature for the Catholic church to be again making its presence felt in the city which had fathered the reforming movement three centuries previously. However, despite the misgivings, the convent thrived and the nuns became familiar figures in the city as they involved themselves in works for the relief of the poor and the sick. Its fine chapel, designed by Gillespie Graham, was opened in the following year with the bells added in 1858. A school is now attached to the convent.

### 27th

**1782:** One of the most remarkable men of his generation, Henry Home, Lord Kames, died at the age of eighty-six. Schooled in the law and versed in letters, he was also an agrarian improver, an historian, and wrote elegantly on the subject of moral philosophy. He also continued to use Scots speech, as did many of his fellow Lords of Session and thus described himself: "I ken very weel that I am the coarsest and most black-a-vised bitch in a the Court o' Session." The judges were a hard-drinking fraternity and thought nothing of tippling heavily during their trials — biscuits would be nibbled and port or claret quaffed while men were sentenced to death. His grim sense of humour is amply displayed by the remark he made when sending a chess-playing friend to the gallows: "Checkmate, Matthew."

# December

28th _____

29th _____

30th _____

# December

## 28th

**1703:** John Fergusson, a tanner and burgess of the city, acquired
the yard and house at the foot of the close that had come to
be called Lochend Close or Little Lochend Close. It had been
occupied originally by William Ferguson of Lochend. The
name had arisen because the house was situated near the loch
in Restalrig, with the owner being referred to, vulgarly, as
Loch-End. Redevelopment in the nineteen-sixties meant
that the close was realigned, but the names of both closes
have been kept in the modern setting. Today Little Lochend
Close forms the entry to Panmure House and both back on to
the Calton cemetery where rest the remains of the parents
and the grandparents of the novelist Robert Louis Stevenson.

## 29th

**1592:** Throughout the sixteenth and seventeenth centuries,
the Royal Mile and its neighbouring closes and wynds became
a mute witness to the frequent "tulzies" — armed fights —
between various notable landed Scottish families. The most
famous was undoubtedly the "Cleanse the Causeway" tulzie
of 1520, between the Douglas and Hamilton families, but there
were other equally notorious and bloodthirsty affairs for which
Edinburgh was the host. Shortly after Christmas in 1592 two
Border families, the Geddes' of Glenhegden and the Tweedies
of Drummelzie, brought their quarrel to a culmination when
Geddes was shot down in the Cowgate while his horse was
being shod, his way of escape having been barred by the kinsmen
of the Drummelzie family.

## 30th

**1818:** One of the most appalling and inhumane executions ever
to have been witnessed in public in Edinburgh took place on a
gibbet erected against the wall of the church of St Giles in
front of the Signet Library. The victim, twenty-three years old
Robert Johnstone, a wretched, simple criminal who had been
convicted of armed robbery, hardly deserved the fate allotted
to him. The gallows had been imperfectly constructed and
Johnstone was able to rest on his tiptoes when the drop fell.
The crowd was roused to a fury and Johnstone was rescued only
to be recaptured, bled by a surgeon to ascertain if he was alive and
then hanged again. The bloody affair had lasted eight hours
and the execution party had to be protected by a Regiment of Foot
from the Castle.

# December

**31st**————————————————————————————

**1878:** Singly, or arm-in-arm, some speechless, others noisy
and quarrelsome, the votaries of the New Year go meandering in
and out and cannoning one against another; and now and again,
one falls and lies as he has fallen. Before night so many have
gone to bed or the police office, that the streets seem almost
clearer. And as *guisards* and *first footers* are now not much
seen except in country places, when once the New Year has
been rung in and proclaimed at the Tron railings, the festivities
begin to find their way indoors and something like quiet
returns to the town. But think, in those piled *lands* of all the
senseless snorers, all the broken heads and empty pockets!
      —Robert Louis Stevenson, *Edinburgh: Picturesque Notes*